# Beginning
# DREAMWORK

BEGINNING DREAMWORK
How to have a conversation with your soul
by Candy Smith

Published by:
SPC BOOKS
*An Imprint of RPJ & Company, Inc.*
Orlando, Florida
Web site: www.rpjandco.com

ISBN-10: 0-9828277-9-2
ISBN-13: 978-0-9828277-9-6

Library of Congress Control Number: 2011936465

Cover and Interior Design:
RPJ & COMPANY, INC.
www.rpjandco.com

Unless otherwise stated all Scripture citations are from the *New Revised Standard Version Bible,* copyright © 1989, Division of Christian Education of the National Council of the Churches of Christ in the United States of America. Used by permission. All rights reserved.

Names have been changed to protect the privacy of individual people mentioned in this journal.

Printed in the United States of America.

Dedicated
to Adrian with gratitude for his
love and support.

*"Our Lord has, in his great mercy, called you and led you to him by the desire of your heart."*

**The Cloud of Unknowing**[1]

*Then I see and write the following:*

*"Now people are coming back in a big ship floating across the sky.*

*The man in the toga has been leisurely goofing off, but sees the big wooden ship and knows he has to prepare and get down to work. They are here."*

**Candy Smith**
**Dream of 2/24/07**

# SPC BOOKS
*An Imprint of RPJ & Company, Inc.*
## ORLANDO, FLORIDA

# Table of Contents

## PART IV - HEALING

## PART V - COMPASSION AND GROWTH

## PART VI – GUIDANCE

## PART VII – INTEGRATION AND ACTION

# CANDY SMITH

# Beginning
# DREAMWORK

*How to have a conversation with your soul*

# *Foreword*

This wonderful book by Candy Smith, so accessible and so compelling, is an invaluable gift to beginning dreamworkers everywhere. Through the narrative of one person's unusually self-aware experience of feeling her way into dreamwork, it lays out for all of us, in non-technical language, the universal process that is set in motion when dreamwork is effectively engaged. In telling her story, she demonstrates, rather than explains, dreamwork's essential nature. Indeed, the reader is very much aware that Smith has not embarked on this work with its lessons in mind, but rather that she is learning them at the same time the reader is. Every day she unwraps a newly delivered package of dreams and synchronicities (meaningful coincidences); and every day she learns new lessons from what she has received. We learn along with her. As the days go by, larger lessons begin to emerge from the accumulated smaller lessons, and sometimes we even spot them before she does.

If it is not Smith who is self-consciously teaching us, then who is it? Where are these lessons coming from? The author is very clear about the answer. It is the Holy Spirit who is in charge here. The Divine. God. Call it what you will, but give it all the credit that such labels imply. There is no question in the author's mind about this source. She knows it in her bones. And anyone who has done dreamwork with this same effectiveness knows it, too. We do not doubt her for a moment, for we have had the same experience of being taught by something that knows more than we do, something that comes to us from beyond space and time and understands our lives better than any mortal, including ourselves, could possibly understand them. This Whatever-It-Is shows us bits of the future before it arrives and reveals aspects of the past that we never knew. It orders our day-by-day dream lessons in just the right way, unfolding a lesson plan that we ourselves never could have authored, for we never imagined that these were the lessons we needed to learn. And yet as we meet each lesson that comes to us, we recognize with awe that this is precisely what we need to understand at this moment, precisely the key that will allow us to move forward on our never-ending, but always fulfilling, journey toward health and wholeness.

And so I reiterate: as strange as it might seem to those who have never been here, this world of expanded meaning is familiar ground for the growing number of people who have learned to do effective dreamwork. And this, of course, raises the question of what exactly it is that makes dreamwork effective. Everyone dreams, but few people are led by their dreams into this surprisingly palpable relationship with the Divine. Why is this? What does it take to get there? Here again Smith teaches without intending to. In simply telling her story, she shows us the answer to this question.

As she embarks on this new venture into dreamwork, she tells us that she tried dreamwork once before, but that she never got much from it. This was a decade or two in the past, in her early middle age, when she turned away from traditional religion to explore alternative paths, including Native American spirituality. During that time, she tells us, she recorded her dreams; but that was all she did with them—she had no systematic way to interpret them. "Occasionally I would have one that gave me helpful information," she writes, "but the majority didn't mean anything to me." Many people have had this experience. I have heard it reported countless times by people who learn of my involvement in dreamwork. "Oh," they say with interest, "I write down my dreams. I've done it for years."

"Do you get much from them?" I ask.

"A little," they say. "Sometimes."

This would not be the answer of someone who is doing effective dreamwork. That answer would be, "Yes, I get a lot from them, all the time."

So simply writing dreams down is not enough. It is indeed the first step, but there are two keys that are needed to turn the mere recollection of dreams into effective dreamwork. The first key is to find a good method of interpretation and then use that method on a regular basis. The problem with this, the sticking point for most of us, is that doing so takes precious time from our day. But then so does brushing our teeth and taking our daily walk. So does preparing a meal and washing the dishes. We don't always like to do these things, and sometimes our resolution falters and we neglect them for a while. But we always return to them because we cannot live well without them. They are key elements in the support of everyday life. And so, too, surprisingly enough, is dreamwork. We don't know this until we have experienced it, but once we do experience it, we find that we cannot turn away from it for any appreciable length of time. It is too important. Too vital. Too essential to the meaning of our lives.

So the first key to effective dreamwork is to regularly employ a good method of dream interpretation. There are many dreamwork methods out there, some of them better than others. In my experience, the methods that have a Jungian basis are the best. Smith got excellent results from the Judeo-Christian, Jungian-based resources she found.[1] The fact that it was a spiritual foundation that laid the groundwork for her successful journey points us toward the second key for effective dreamwork. These are like the two keys that are needed for a safe-deposit box. The dreamwork method corresponds to the individual key that each of us has for our own box. It is essential. We cannot get into the box without it. But that one key will not get us in unless the bank's master key is used along with it. For effective dreamwork, the master key is a faith tradition. For Smith, the faith tradition is Christianity, but it does not have to be that. It can be Judaism, Islam, Buddhism, Taoism, or any other religious tradition that encourages the ego to bow its head to the Ultimate Mystery, the Source, the Oneness, the All-Merciful, the All-Loving, the Eternal, or any other name we want to use for the transcendent aspect of God.

In Jungian-Christian writings, including my own, God's transcendent aspect is understood to be the masculine aspect of the Divine. In contrast, the immanent aspect of God that we encounter in dreams and synchronicity— indeed, in all the flow of life—is understood to be the feminine aspect of the Divine. The literate world's faith traditions have specialized in the masculine side of our human spiritual potential, while for the most part they have carried very little consciousness of spirituality's feminine side. Conversely, the pre-literate world's native traditions have specialized in the feminine side of our human spirituality, while carrying very little consciousness of the masculine side. The challenge for our time is to join these two sides together, for each is enriched and completed by the other.

This challenge emerges as a central theme in this book, although Smith herself does not have a concept of it in these terms as she embarks on the work. All she knows is that she has a problem to work out between the revival in her dreams of her earlier interest in Native American spirituality and her unwillingness to jeopardize the life-giving relationship she has more recently established with traditional Christianity. Only at the end of her story does she come to see how these two streams of her spiritual potential fit together. Through following both her faith and her dreams, she lives into the answer to a problem that more and more of us are facing, whether we give it this name or not: the problem of reconciling the masculine and feminine sides of our human spirituality. The author's demonstration through the course of this book of what this solution looks like is far more effective than any didactic discourse about it could ever be. Not that her solution looks exactly the same as anyone else's would, but the basic, shared elements of the universal solution are there. And these elements are, in a nutshell, faith and dreams.

I myself had a dream that gave me these two words— "faith" and "dreams"—for the essence of the two sides of human spirituality. Before I dreamed this dream, back in 2001, I never would have known that these two words were sufficient to define the crux of it all. It is not that the dream said, nor do I believe, that these two words are exhaustive. Both the masculine and feminine sides of our spirituality have much more to them than any two words alone can cover. But for the essence of the two sides, says the dream, and I agree, they are sufficient. Here is the dream:

I WAS TRYING TO EXPLAIN THE ESSENCE OF SPIRITUAL LIFE TO SOME PEOPLE IN A CHURCH SETTING. "IT CONSISTS OF TWO PARTS," I SAID. THE PEOPLE WERE INTERESTED IN THAT—THEY WERE LISTENING. I ESPECIALLY NOTICED A WOMAN PRIEST WITH SHORT, STRAIGHT HAIR—A TYPE, NOT SOMEONE I ACTUALLY KNEW. AS I BEGAN THIS PRESENTATION, WE WERE NEAR THE END OF OUR SESSION AND ALMOST OUT OF TIME.

"ONE PART IS THE LIFE OF FAITH," I SAID, REALIZING AT THAT MOMENT THAT *FAITH* IS THE ESSENCE OF THE MASCULINE SIDE.

YES, YES! THEY ALL AGREED WITH THAT ENTHUSIASTICALLY. THE TIME FOR THE SESSION WAS ENDING. VERY HAPPY AND SATISFIED, THEY ALL GOT UP TO LEAVE. THEY DID NOT EVEN NOTICE THAT I HAD NOT YET HAD A CHANCE TO TELL THEM ABOUT THE SECOND PART. EVEN THE WOMAN PRIEST CARED ONLY ABOUT THE FAITH SIDE OF OUR LIFE WITH GOD.

I WENT OUT TO WHERE THEY WERE NOW STANDING ABOUT. "YOU DIDN'T HEAR THE SECOND PART," I SAID. THEY HAD TO ADMIT THEY HAD NOT, AND SO THEY GAVE ME THEIR HALF-HEARTED ATTENTION.

"THE SECOND PART IS DREAMS," I SAID. I HAD THOUGHT THIS THROUGH BEFORE SAYING IT. I HAD

SORTED THROUGH ALL THE VARIOUS ELEMENTS AND
EXPRESSIONS OF THE FEMININE SIDE OF SPIRITUALITY
AND HAD REALIZED THAT *DREAMS* ARE THE ESSENCE OF
THE FEMININE SIDE, AS *FAITH* IS OF THE MASCULINE.

"TO LIVE A WHOLE RELIGIOUS LIFE," I SAID, "YOU
NEED TO THINK ABOUT AND RECORD YOUR DREAMS AT
LEAST TWICE A WEEK. EVERY DAY WOULD BE BETTER, BUT
TWICE A WEEK IS THE MINIMUM." I SAID THIS AFTER
THINKING ABOUT IT AND CONCLUDING THAT CHURCH
PEOPLE IN GENERAL COULD ONLY BE EXPECTED TO
RECORD DREAMS TWICE A WEEK.

This is one of those rare dreams that is largely self-explanatory. Besides teaching me that the two sides of our life with God can be summed up in these two words, it also made clear that even the presence of women in the clergy was not making a difference (in 2001) in institutional Christianity's recognition of the feminine aspect of God. It would have been one thing if I had awakened from this dream and compared it with my actual experience in outer life and seen that the dream scenario did not compute. Then I would have said: *No, there really is more interest than that when I share with my fellow church people what I have learned about the importance of dreams and synchronicity.* In this case the dream would have been a picture of my fears, not of reality.

But that was not the conclusion that came from comparing the dream scenario to outer life. Rather, the conclusion was: *Yes, this is exactly what it feels like when I try to tell my fellow church-going Christians about what I have learned about the two sides of our life with God. Only a very few laypeople are interested in hearing anything about it, and even fewer clergy.* Therefore the dream was saying: you are not mistaken about how your words are being received—and even worse, the women clergy, who you thought would be more open to this, are not. But note that the dream does contain a ray of hope. My dreamself follows the uninterested audience out into the hall and challenges them, on the basis of fairness, to hear me out. And on that basis they do listen further, though not with enthusiasm. The dream does not say what happens after they hear the message. But there is hope in the fact that my dreamself is already adjusting the requirements for dreamwork to what I know will be practical for institutional Christians.

Every day more and more people walk away from their faith traditions because of the very problem shown in this dream: the one-sided skew of those traditions toward masculine spirituality. Few of the disaffected understand their estrangement in these terms. They simply know in their gut, in their core, that something is wrong here, that too much of what is vital in life is being left out. Times have changed in the last fifty years. Feminine life energies are now much more accepted in the world at large than they used to be. Sexuality, feelings, dreams, mystical perceptions, feeling the flow and going with it—all these unruly but potentially creative and wisdom-producing components of our human nature have been released from centuries—even millennia—of repression. It was an overly zealous faith that repressed them. And yet now that they have found their way out into the light, it is, ironically, faith itself—albeit a more open and courageous faith— that is the master key for unlocking their true potential.

This is what this book is about. The problem rises to the fore at the beginning of Smith's story and remains prominent all the way through. She loves the new home she has found in traditional Christianity, and she intends to stay there. But her own nature, her own spirit, is greater than the limited context for spiritual growth that institutional Christianity provides. In order to be true to herself, she has to allow her own understanding of God the Father, Christ, and the Holy Spirit to be expanded beyond the traditional, institutional bounds of understanding.

More and more individuals are being called to recognize the feminine side of spirituality and hold it together with the masculine side. Smith was called to this challenge out of the blue, with no idea, at first, of what was being asked of her. I was called to it in the same way. So, too, have many others been; and so, too, will many others be as time goes on. As Smith recognizes so clearly, this is the Holy Spirit at work among us; it is not our own doing! It is my belief, my hope, that our faith traditions will eventually expand to catch up with us, as humanity as a whole comes to understand more and more clearly what spiritual wholeness, the union of the masculine and feminine divine, is all about. It is, simply put, about faith and dreams. Not just faith. Not just dreams. Faith *and* dreams. Together. A couple. A marriage.

Read on and see for yourself what rich fruit is produced by the marriage of the masculine and feminine divine in an individual human life.

*- Joyce Rockwood Hudson*
*August 16, 2010*

# Acknowledgments

Thank you, Joyce Rockwood Hudson, for suggesting that I turn the manuscript into a journal. It sent me on a whole new journey that uncovered more gems in the dreamwork process. I am extremely grateful for your insight, extensive editorial support, and a very gracious Foreword.

Thank you, Jodi Werling, for the months of editing work, for helping me fill in the gaps in my story, for making my writing coherent—making me sound much better than I ever could, and for becoming a close friend.

Thank you, Kathy Schubitz, for the long hours you spent in teaching me what it takes to turn hand-written words into a book. You have encouraged me, prayed for me, and you even taught me more about how to use my computer.

Thank you, Sharey Biles and Glee Krentz, for the hours and hours you both spent proofreading and helping me clarify and make my writing more understandable.

Thank you, Kathy Lowry. If you hadn't taken an interest in the manuscript—reading it, brainstorming with me, and referring me to Kathy Schubitz—it might never have been published.

A special thanks to the Spirit Scribes writing class and to my Bible study friends for their feedback and their friendship in Christ.

And especially, thank you, Adrian. You have been a patient and supportive companion, always encouraging me in this endeavor. May we share many more dreams together!

Most of all, thank you Holy Spirit and Native American friends on the other side for lifting the veil and helping me see the symbols through the silvery light of the moon, and for guiding this journey from the beginning to the end. Thank you for steering me toward Home.

# Beginning
# DREAMWORK

*God has arranged all things in the world
in consideration of everything else.*

*. . . everything that is in the heavens,
on the earth, and under the earth,
is penetrated with connectedness,
is penetrated with relatedness.*

**Hildegard of Bingen**[1]

*. . . in the shadow of your wings
I will take refuge . . .*

**Psalm 57:1**[2]

*The inner journey, pursued faithfully and well,
always takes us back to the world of action.*

**Parker J. Palmer**[3]

# Introduction

In June 2007 I was scheduled to present a workshop on dreams and dreamwork at our "Faith in Arts" weekend at my church. During the previous five months I had been on a spiritual journey through dreams that had taken me on a deep exploration of myself and my relationship with the Divine. This book is the culmination of that journey. Through my dreams, the dreamwork process, and synchronistic events, I was given new insight into a world of *meaning* and the many signs that God gives to guide and affirm us.

A few weeks before the workshop, I found a slightly injured baby female cowbird near my house and brought her home. I put her in a paper bag and set her in a dark, quiet place as a friend once told me to do with birds that fly into windows. Later, when she seemed to have recovered from being in shock, my husband Adrian and I returned her to the spot where I had found her. We had no idea if her parents would find her or if she would survive.

The morning of the dream workshop, I dreamed that a small gray bird flew to me as I rested in a chair and put its feet on my mouth. Then it nestled next to my right cheek. It seemed to be a clear sign that what I would be doing that day was being blessed by the Divine! A passage that I often heard our diaconal minister, Susan, quote from Psalm 19 came to mind: "Let the words of my mouth and the meditation of my heart be acceptable to you, O LORD, my rock and my redeemer."[4]

Through my dream journey, I had been shown by the Holy Spirit that I was to share my dreamwork experience, but to what extent hadn't been made clear. After the gray bird dream, I felt reassured that I was on the right track, and I was grateful for the affirmation.

As I played the guitar that morning for the opening service of the "Faith in Arts" workshop, we heard a knocking sound at the window in the front of the church, behind the altar. When we finished the final song, I left my guitar in the back and went to investigate. There, hopping against the window, was a female cowbird! I felt again that I was being given confirmation that I was doing what the weeks of dreamwork had prepared me to do. I thanked God for this beautiful affirmation.

A couple of hours later, as I began my presentation in one of the conference rooms, the little bird pecked at the window directly behind me! This was the third affirmation that morning! Any hesitation I had about relating how God speaks to us in dreams, and how we can develop a closer relationship with the Holy Spirit through dreams, dissolved.

The next day, a friend who knew nothing of what had happened with the bird the day before, said she felt compelled to give me a gift she found at the Arts Festival. She said she *knew* it was meant for me. The gift was a wooden plaque with a painting of a bird's nest and the words "Bless Our Nest." I was awed—a fourth affirmation that sharing this journey was what the Holy Spirit intended!

◈◈

This book is about contrasts and balance, about the interconnectedness of all things that exist, from God down to the tiniest pebble. It's about the web that connects everything. Join me and learn about the inner and outer world, the spiritual and the physical, about the feminine and the masculine, about brokenness and wholeness, and about fragmentation and integration.

If anyone had asked me before this journey, about pursuing dreams as a spiritual practice, and about whether spending two to three hours a day recording and interpreting dreams was worthwhile, I might have questioned the wisdom of this path. The path didn't cost any money, but it exacted a price. I found that it only worked when I had a passionate desire to know the Holy Spirit better, and when I was willing to do the work necessary to understand and follow the guidance given. In many ways, I found its wisdom to be stricter than what parents, conscience, and religious systems expect. It was not easy, but it was worth it. It took time and commitment. It was enlightening, comical, and awe-inspiring! This path provided help with everyday situations as well as life's directions. It stirred up difficult memories and, through creative stories, healed me and gave me insight into the deepest levels of my being.

What I hope to do in the following pages is to shine a small light by recounting my own initiation into deeply meaningful dreamwork. I share it through journaling so you can see how the dreamwork unfolded—how I learned and stumbled, but ultimately healed through the process. The format has helped me reveal it more like a story, which has made it richer for me, as I hope it will be for you.

As I share my journey, sometimes you may find that I don't explain every dream symbol nor do I include every dream. This is because I either didn't see or didn't understand the meaning in those dreams and symbols. But I've learned that it's okay! The same dream can keep unfolding over days, weeks, months, and even years. The same or similar symbols will reappear if there is more to learn about them and about ourselves. A dream gives us what we need even if can't remember all of it. It's not necessary to carefully analyze every piece to get it all right. What is important is the unfolding process, the shift inside that wants to be known. It is more a dance with the dreams than it is a scientific dissection. The blossoming of our consciousness is in *us*, not in the dreams. The dreams are prompts, which, when worked with just enough, keep the new understandings coming.

Through Dreamwork you can learn to communicate with and understand your very soul. With that, you can attain the balance necessary to have healthy relationships in your life—with other people, the natural world, and with the Divine.

*It is in that light and with thankfulness to the Creator for the shelter of his wing at night that I share this path with those who desire to know the Holy Spirit and themselves better.*

*- Candy Smith*

# PART 1

# DISCERNMENT

Chapter 1

# Who Am I?

To understand my dream journey as it unfolds in the following pages, it will help to know a bit about me and the experiences and people that have shaped my life.

First of all, this world of dreams is new for me. Understanding metaphors, allegories, parables, and the like have never been easy for me—I even struggle to understand the stories Jesus told. I am just an ordinary person set here on God's earth. Simply put, my role is that of a wife, mother, and grandmother.

❧

Growing up in Mariemont, Ohio in the 1950s was a happy time. The parents on my street were great friends who took turns sitting on each other's patio in warm weather. While dinner cooked, they would enjoy a beer, martini, or whiskey sour while we children played. My parents chose bourbon and water. Later, many of the neighbors sipped nightcaps while watching Johnny Carson. This was the suburban lifestyle then. When one of the neighbors drank to excess, it was spoken of in hush-hush tones, with a shake of the head, while Desi and Lucy kept everyone laughing.

Although I felt secure in this fifties American life, I had a childlike insecurity and a fear of disappointing my parents. At the age of four, I threw sand in another child's eyes. While my parents didn't deal with me harshly, I remember being concerned that I had disappointed them. Even as a teenager, I remember sitting at the top of the stairs at night listening to my parents' conversation in the living room below, to see if they would say anything critical of me. While most children outgrow this insecurity, I have carried it with me throughout my life—in the workplace, in my marriage, friendships, and my relationship with God.

About the time my twelfth birthday came around, several significant things happened. My sister, Judy (my only sibling), left for college, and my parents could no longer afford the house we had lived in for the last six years. To deal with the anxiety and stress, my father began to stop for drinks on his way home from work, something he had never done before. When he arrived home later, he acted silly—not himself. He was never mean or abusive, just drunk. Mom never said much. She kept that code of honor. We learned that it was useless to talk to Dad when he was like that because he never remembered our conversations the next morning.

When my parents returned home late from a night out dancing or playing bridge, and it sounded like they had been drinking, I would tiptoe from my bed and quietly throw up in the bathroom. They were loving parents, but when they drank too much, it was obvious something was different about them and I felt quite alone.

In order to cope with this temporary abandonment, I fantasized that my beloved TV cowboys and Indians befriended me and I became their little partner. I wrote to "Little Joe," a character played by Michael Landon on the

TV series *Bonanza*, and told him about my dad's drinking, but all I got back was an 8 x 10 glossy. I had daydreams about rescuing Baby Jesus—an attempt to take care of the frightened child that I had become. I made a vow never to let my own children see me drunk. This difficult time was the beginning of panic attacks, something I wouldn't understand until my late thirties.

Unfortunately, the patterns that were set during my impressionable childhood years were carried into my adult life. Having taken care of myself when I felt abandoned by my parents' drinking gave me strength, but it also forged that "don't tell anyone" attitude that kept inner conflicts locked inside for years. Never having learned to talk through or get help for problems meant that I stayed too long with the status quo when things went wrong in my twenty-seven-year marriage. My difficulties were not visible to the average friend; I followed the "don't tell" rule and adhered to the cultural norm of honoring my spouse by keeping my marital difficulties a secret.

In 1995 when my son, Rob, and my daughter, Kelly, were both away at college, my marriage to their father, Tim, finally ended. But the issues from my childhood and from that marriage stayed with me, and it is through the dreamwork I am sharing in this volume that I was forced to face them head-on.

శోన్

The dysfunction of my own life is, sadly, not unique. I have been thinking about this in regard to my mother. When she turned eighty, I asked her if she would write stories from her childhood. She rarely talked about her family. She was the youngest of seven children and was usually thrust into the care of older siblings so her mom could help her dad in their Indiana restaurant. Mom always said that her childhood memories were unhappy ones. Nevertheless, she took on the challenge. While caring for my ailing father, she filled a binder with wonderful hand-written stories about my aunts, uncles, grandparents, and life in the 1920s and 1930s. When she was finished, she shared with me that writing down these stories had shown her that she had indeed had a happy childhood after all. She learned that she had fond memories of her family and growing up in that tiny rural Midwestern town.

It wasn't until after her death that my sister and I found some other stories that she had written down but had not shown us. She wrote of how she was date-raped by a young man with whom her father had fixed her up. This occurred in the same year, at age nineteen, that her father made her break up with her non-Catholic boyfriend whom she loved, and that she lost her mother. No wonder she didn't want to look back! These were sad and painful stories that she always kept private. Yet, she did record them; she must have wanted us to know about them.

Mom's sad stories speak of a child who missed her mother dearly, first because my grandmother worked long hours, and then because of her untimely death. Mom was so influenced by her strong German father that she was never able to assert herself and take action even in minor situations. Her life story tells of a violent break with her feminine side through losing her mother and being overpowered by the masculine (her father and the rapist).

Because of *her* childhood, Mom wasn't capable of taking a stand against Dad's drinking, even though it must have felt like she had lost her life's companion. His nightly drinking went on for over twenty-five years and she quietly put up with it. Her seething inner anger made their lives as difficult as his drinking did. In thinking through these memories, I see why she wasn't able to figure out how to help me, or anyone else, in deeply troubling situations. At about age nine, I furiously rode my bike home to tell her that a man at the gas station (where I had put air in my tires) had just asked me how I knew I was a girl. He kept insisting that I answer him. I might not have been the brightest bear in the woods, but I sure knew that he was up to no good. I got out of there quickly and went to Mom for some explanation about this uncomfortable encounter. Her only comment was that I should have told him that after I was born, I had "pink booties"! I didn't know what she meant, but I knew, at some level, that she just didn't know how to deal with this situation.

She couldn't help me process or validate my feelings, or talk about how to protect myself from a would-be predator. Her disregard of my emotional state made me question my own feelings. She was a loving mother in many ways, but she passed on to us this painful separation from vital feminine feeling and wisdom. She couldn't do otherwise.

കൗൽ

We were raised Roman Catholic—my parents went to church every Sunday and Holy Day of their lives. The Catholic traditions, Catholic grade school, and singing the Latin masses were all a comforting and grounding part of my early years.

My dad had been Lutheran and converted to Catholicism shortly after he and Mom were married. At age fifteen I posed questions to my dad about some difficulties I was having with certain Catholic beliefs. I have since forgotten what the difficulties were, but I remember that he was upset and said he would send me to Bishop Sheen (a popular television personality), who could straighten me out!

Like many teenagers, while at college, I attended church sporadically, sometimes only on Christmas and Easter. It was the late 1960s, and I was open to new-age thinking. Beginning at this time and far into my adult life, I read about Buddhism and Taoism, loved folk music, learned meditation, and thought I was enlightened. But the truth is . . . I was about as lost as a sheep could get. I was always in search of something, but didn't know exactly what. I was looking in the wrong places at times but was smart enough to know that it had to do with God and finding a "home."

Most of my professional years were spent as a social service supervisor in a children's protective service agency. The work involved looking at facts, problem-solving, setting a course of action, writing and implementing grants, and working on endless statistics and budgets. Oftentimes my schedule and activities were sometimes planned a year or two in advance. In my work, I believed the Divine had a special heart for children and that the Holy Spirit helped those of us doing the difficult children's protective work. But, I felt disconnected from my religious roots. I began studying and meditating on Native American themes. Learning about Indian life and culture was fascinating, and the meditations calming. I also took a Silva meditation class a number of times and experienced the sacredness and interconnectedness of all life. But from 1987 to 2003 I was about as far from traditional religion as a believer could get.

A part of me kept wondering if there was something more . . . something just seemed to be missing. I felt that if I could just find the way to access, to see, to *connect* with that Something which seemed just beyond my grasp, life might be more understandable . . . relevant . . . meaningful.

When my parents died in 2003—Mom first, then Dad eight months later—I missed them but felt blessed to have been with them toward the end of their lives and when they passed. When Dad died in October, I had this strange thirst to read books about and by religious figures like St. Paul and St. Luke. I couldn't get enough of C.S. Lewis, Teilhard de Chardin, Tozer, and others.

While sitting on my couch on a quiet winter night in February, 2004, after finishing Lee Strobel's *A Case for Christ*, something happened. My struggles ended. I quit running away. I felt caught up in loving arms. In a stream of joyful tears, I surrendered to the Christ I had known and been skirting all my life—the Christ I had kept at a safe distance. Safe so nothing would be asked of me, so I could be in control of my own life, or so I thought!

In the months to come, I joined the local Lutheran Church, married Adrian, the anchor and love of my life, and ingested book after holy book. My spirit was starving to know more of the Divine. I was in love with Christ, Christianity, and the Bible. With the friends at my Lutheran Church and the pastor's weekly direction in the Sunday service and Wednesday morning Bible study, I felt safe, secure and loved. The marriage of my Catholic roots and this new Lutheran theology, in my mind, was a perfect blend.

But . . . here's the point: I was still doing it all. I was in control of what ministries I joined, of what I read, and of what Bible study classes I took. I was still making it all about me and what I wanted to know and learn. I had surrendered, but I hadn't fully allowed God to be the ship's captain, the caller of the dance—(see, I'm getting a little better at this metaphor thing). It wasn't until a special day in 2007, when I took my "rainbow walk" and asked the Divine to teach me to do God's will, that my life started to change. That's when this new dreamwork started. Prior to that, my experience in working with my dreams was limited to a long-ago attempt at keeping a daily account of them. I had also read a variety of books about dreams, but had never followed through with any meaningful dream interpretation. When, in early 2007, I realized I was on a dream journey led by the Holy Spirit. . . I was as startled as anyone!

*We affirm the importance of the Church's values,*
*beliefs, and teachings.*
*Nevertheless, they cannot be substituted for direct and*
*living experience of the presence of God.*
*Will we listen?*
*Will we allow original material to enter our lives?*
**Louis M. Savary, Patricia H. Berne, and Strephon**
**Kaplan Williams**[1]

*If you abide in me, and my words abide in you,*
*Ask for whatever you wish,*
*and it will be done for you.*
**John 15:7**[2]

*It is learning to trust that God is in the center of the*
*circle of our lives, in the center of our hearts.*
*We can count on that Presence which makes itself*
*known through feelings, dreams, and synchronicities.*
*Intuition is a natural state of consciousness in which*
*our small isolated mind opens up to the*
*Big Mind of the Divine.*
**Joan Borysenko**[3]

Chapter 2

# A Matter of Faith

Dream: *Tink*

## December 20, 2006

Even in retirement (for real this time!) it is still difficult to get up each day and just be. I find myself thinking back, looking for that peaceful, beautiful, apartment I dreamed about two years ago. The lighting, the colors, the furnishings evoke a peacefulness I've never really known. To remember it still fills me with warmth, love, and a sense of being home. I yearn to be there—to dwell in that beautiful place. I have been trying to get there, but I am just not there yet.

Today, though, something powerful happened and I feel a sense of hope! During my waking hours early this morning, a winter storm was rolling in and I could hear high winds whipping through our pine trees. My body was fighting a cold and my joints ached, so I rolled over to go back to sleep. I had no intention of going on my morning walk. As I lay in bed, asking the Lord to take the virus away so I could sing the cantor part in the church choir, I heard in my head: "Watch for the blue; go on your walk." *Are you serious? It's totally gray, windy, and rainy!* But, I noticed a brightening outside. When I pulled myself out of that warm bed and looked out my window to the east I could see the sky was turning blue. It was almost sunrise. "Go on your walk; you will laugh!" What else could I do? *Okay, Lord . . . I trust you.*

As usual, the Lord decided my agenda. As I walked my familiar route up the road and into the sunrise, I thought of how I have been struggling to understand how to have a relationship with Him. It was bright blue in the east, with a brilliant golden sun peeking through the clouds, but there was a strong wind and I could see gray and black clouds in the west, coming my way. Knowingly, I had to trust Him, because it looked like I could really end up in a downpour. And yet, as soon as the thought entered my mind, I knew God would protect me. In looking back to the west, I saw a vertical rainbow! I walked backwards into the sunrise and for the next ten minutes I watched as rainbow after rainbow appeared. When I thought He couldn't amaze me more, a double rainbow appeared! Laugh? My heart wanted to break it was so beautiful—those bright rainbows in the black sky with our neighborhood all green and lit up by the golden light of that early morning sun.

As I rounded the last corner, the wind picked up and blew me down the street with the leaves. I was laughing! Free! I felt no worry about my cold or the rain or what would happen tomorrow.

Words can't adequately describe this *kairos*[4] moment. I see now that the topic this morning wasn't just about my *relationship* with God, but about *trust*. When I heeded the message, "Watch for the blue," and followed, I trusted, and know now that I have to learn, in every part of my life, to let go of wanting to know what is next, what the plans are—wanting to be in control. I have to trust and let the Holy Spirit call the shots.

## January 26, 2007

This morning, I dreamed that Mom came for a visit. I was so excited to see her—it's been almost four years since she passed away. I asked if she would come back to visit me again. She replied, *"IT'S A MATTER OF FAITH!"* To which I defensively said, *"BUT, I BELIEVE!"* I was hurt and confused that she was questioning my faith. I have always believed in God, even during those many years I didn't attend church. But, lately I have found myself on a path of wanting to grow my relationship with the Divine, to learn more. Perhaps in order to do that, I have to figure out what she meant by those words.

ॐ

## February 8, 2007

I don't know what it is, but I'm feeling as if my dreams are more meaningful, or important, lately. Something feels different. Am I simply more aware of them or are they simply more interesting? It's been almost two weeks since I dreamed of Mom and I keep thinking of what she said in the dream.

In this morning's dream, I took a woman on a walking journey that led us to a crossroad and through four quadrants. When I woke from the dream, I drew a picture of the crossroads and the four quadrants. The result was a sort of map.

If I picture myself standing in the map, at the crossroads facing south, I can apply what I remember from reading about dreams and even from my prior dream experiences: Dreaming of turning to my right, and seeing dream objects on my right, refer to the outer physical world; turning to my left, and objects on my left, refer to the inner unconscious world, proceeding all the way to Carl Jung's "collective unconscious."[5] But, I have never seen the concepts of *chronos* vs. *kairos* time, earth world vs. spirit world, consciousness vs. unconsciousness, and space/time vs. non-space/time mapped out in detail like this! I believe the intersection of the crossroads and all four quadrants are accessible to everyone, although most of the time we are only aware of the lower right quadrant.

Why are there two dream quadrants: one in the earthly unconscious half, and the other in the spiritual unconscious half? Could it be that some dreams are more ordinary while some are what Carl Jung terms "archetypal"[6] dreams? In the Archetypal Dreams quadrant of the map is a turquoise ball in the midst of a bush. The ball has a yin-yang design. I have no idea what this might mean.

I'm fascinated! Why was I given this information and what am I to do with it?

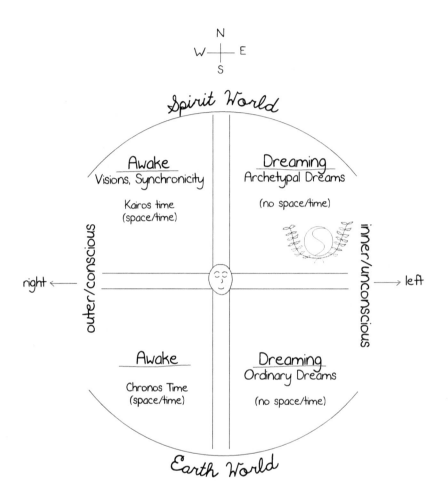

## February 10, 2007

Today would have been Dad's 90th birthday.

This morning I woke with a start, as if I had been rudely booted out of dreamland. I realized I hadn't been breathing; my heart was skipping beats, my chest hurt, and I was out of breath. While I was coming to consciousness, I heard someone say, *"You okay, Tink?"* I was confused. Was someone asking about me?

When I was fully awake, I thought about it and realized that the only *"TINK"* I know is Tinker Bell from Peter Pan. Why would someone ask *TINK* if she was okay? I remembered—in the play, Tinker Bell *was* sick—maybe dying! Peter turns to the audience of frightened children and tells them if they believe, to clap their hands; to not let *TINK* die.[7] Does this have something to do with my mother's assertion that *IT'S A MATTER OF FAITH?* Can having a closer relationship with God possibly be as simple as clapping and shouting "I believe"?

Last night I was tired and not particularly excited about starting the book we are using for Bible study. It's by Beth Moore, entitled *Believing God*. This morning, as I thought about the *TINK* dream, I remembered a sentence in the introduction of the book: "Faith happens when believers believe."[8] When reading the next sentence, I felt as if I had jumped into her shoes: "I thought I had plenty of faith. After all, how much faith does a church-going, church-serving soul need? I would soon learn the answer: a whole lot more than I had."[9] Exactly! Even though I have been attending church and Bible study regularly for these past three years and have joined so many ministries, in my imagination I feel as if I am being urged to join in with the children from *Peter Pan*, to clap and yell, "I believe!" More than anything I want my faith to grow stronger in the same way that Tinker Bell's golden fairy light grew brighter on stage.

In *Believing God*, Moore refers to Isaiah 43, and I was held fast by the prophet's words:

> *You are my witnesses, says the Lord and my servant*
> *whom I have chosen so that you may know and believe*

*me . . . I have called you by name and you are mine . . . Do*
*not remember the former things or consider the things of*
*old. I am about to do a NEW THING; now it springs*
*forth, do you not perceive it? . . . you are precious in my*
*sight and honored, and I love you . . .* [10]

I feel as if I am on some kind of spiritual journey now.
First the "rainbow walk," then the dream of Mom's visit,
the Quadrants Map dream, and this morning's TINK
dream. I believe all dreams are from God and it feels as if I
am being called to faith at a whole new level, a journey to
get to know God, and myself, better. The lessons seem to
be coming closer together, as if the teaching is intensifying.
If I believe the messages from Mom and Isaiah, I have
work to do. It appears that there is more to faith, trust, and
belief than I yet know. And dreams seem to be a vehicle
provided by the Holy Spirit for learning, if I am willing to
get on board!

I do want to follow these teachings with faith—"I
believe!" But, I'm scared to venture into this new realm,
this realm of *meaning* where things work so differently
from the logical ways I am used to. Am I willing to risk
this journey?

How can I not?

*. . . we are in constant touch with a world that is
as real to us while we are in it, and has as much to
do with who we are, and whose ultimate origin and
destiny are as unknown and fascinating
as the world of waking reality . . .
our lives are a great deal richer, deeper, more
intricately interrelated, more mysterious, and less
limited by time
and space than we commonly suppose.*

**Frederick Buechner[1]**

*Indeed you delight in truth deep within me,
and would have me know wisdom deep within.*

**Psalm 51:6[2]**

*Spirituality is about emergence, surpassing old forms
and old thinking, revealing hidden potential
opening the mind to new ways of seeing,
attaining more than affirmation,
and seeing more than what has already been seen.*

**Lee Irwin[3]**

Chapter 3

# Dreamwork Techniques

Dreams: *Mom's Visit; The Monopoly Game/Indian Head*
Vision: *The Indian Head*

## February 12, 2007

Today I bought a tiny flashlight and taped it to a pen so I can write down my dreams in the night without disturbing Adrian. This will work much better than using a tape recorder like I did when I tried recording my dreams while the kids were in high school. Now I won't have to spend time transcribing the dreams; they'll be written down and waiting for me when I am ready to work on them.

When I think about that first attempt at doing dreamwork, I realize my failure to follow any systematic way of interpreting the dreams, so most of them seemed unintelligible. I remember there were a few that were helpful, but the majority just didn't seem to mean anything.

After the dreams of the past few weeks, I have come to accept that I am being offered an opportunity to fulfill my desire to grow my faith. In light of that, I feel as if I need a framework—a Christian framework—for decoding the dreams. So, today I searched my bookshelves and pulled out several of my Christian-based dream books—the ones I have already read—then searched the Internet and found a new one. I'm hoping that if I study them, I will learn some systematic way of working with my dreams.

**February 18, 2007**

The knowledge and encouragement gained from reviewing all of the books[4] helped me lay out a system to work with my dreams. Today, I tried it out on my *Mom's Visit* dream from three weeks ago:

**1. After waking from a dream, write it down.**

*I SEE MOM. SHE IS SITTING NEXT TO ME ON MY RIGHT AT A TABLE. IN FRONT OF HER IS A PIECE OF WALNUT LAYER CAKE AND OTHER DESSERTS. I STAND NEXT TO HER HOLDING A BOWL OF OATMEAL. AS I LOOK IN MY LITTLE BOWL, THE OATMEAL DISAPPEARS, THEN REAPPEARS AGAIN. WHEN I LOOK UP, MOM IS STANDING ON THE OTHER SIDE OF THE TABLE LOOKING AT ME. I AM SO HAPPY TO SEE HER, AND I ASK IF SHE WILL VISIT ME AGAIN. SHE SAYS, "IT'S A MATTER OF FAITH." I AM SURPRISED AND HURT AND SAY, "BUT, I BELIEVE!"*

**2. Write down every detail I can remember.**

Include objects, colors, spatial arrangement, what is said, the story line, feelings, how things change or move, what my involvement is, any detail—even on dream characters' clothes or on a table, etc . . . I wrote TABLE, OATMEAL; MOM is sitting ON MY RIGHT; I AM SURPRISED AND HURT; OATMEAL DISAPPEARS, THEN REAPPEARS; CAKE is a WALNUT LAYER CAKE.

## 3. Give the dream a title.

Use the content from the dream to give it a title that will help me remember the dream—in this case, MOM'S VISIT.

## 4. Determine the general idea of the dream.

Mom's statement, "IT'S A MATTER OF FAITH," makes it pretty evident that this dream is asking me to delve into what it really means to have FAITH. It's been three years since I immersed myself in reading and prayer and began asking God to help me understand Him better—to help me strengthen my relationship with Him. I think Mom's rhetorical statement is the answer to my question! It challenges me to find out what *faith* is all about. I find it significant that she is the messenger, since I am learning that *faith* and a closer connection to the Divine are about being in a *relationship* with Spirit. Who better to lead the way into that exploration than my own mother?

I don't know if the meanings of subsequent dreams will be this easy to figure out, (I have a feeling they won't) but for this one, the main theme seems clear.

## 5. List all symbols from the dream.

MOM, TABLE, OATMEAL, MATTER OF FAITH, etc. A dream symbol can be a word, image, action, or even a melody. I know the content of my daily life is often woven into my dreams; dream images might be things I experienced in outer life the day prior to the actual dream. The books all emphasize that this is why the dreamer is the best person to interpret and give meaning to the dream.

**6. List as many questions as I can about the dream and dream images.**

I wrote these questions on the *back* of the list of symbols: "Who is MOM? What does she look like? What does the room look like? What is on the TABLE in this dream? What is my feeling at first seeing her? How does my emotional state change? Where is MOM physically placed in the dream? Why is she placed on the right? Does she move, and if so, in which direction? Why oatmeal vs. cake? Why does the oatmeal disappear then reappear? What does she mean by 'IT'S A MATTER OF FAITH?' What is the MATTER she is referring to?"

**7. Write the answers to the questions.**

I just let my thoughts flow and wrote down everything I could think of: "Maybe Mom is on the right because this dream is pointing to an outer action or event. Oatmeal is something I eat for breakfast as opposed to after dinner. Does the oatmeal appear then disappear to signify that I should pay attention to this symbol? Am I simply being reminded that I should eat more grains for my health? Maybe MOM has CAKE (I love her walnut layer cake) and I have OATMEAL because I need to lay off the sweets and eat healthy food. Or maybe I am in the early process (breakfast) of some adventure that will lead to the end reward (dessert)?

The questions/answers that appeared significant were underlined. It was fantastic—the dream message really did start to unfold! Some answers didn't seem to hit the mark, but with others I got an *Aha!* feeling—the feeling that something is true and has meaning for me. I think the *Aha!* feeling is the Holy Spirit's affirmation that I am on the right track!

I think this step will be my basis for defining what meaning the individual dream figures, images, and symbols have for me and what lesson I am supposed to learn . . . Jeremy Taylor and others involved in dreamwork believe that dreams never come just to tell what is already known.[5] They come to heal, to give insight and guidance, and to make us whole— physically, psychologically, and spiritually.[6]

**8. Write what the symbols represent.**

I turned back to my list of symbols on the *front* of the page and wrote the meanings next to the symbol. For MOM I wrote, "My own maternal voice, an image that guides or challenges me."

In one of the books I reviewed, it stated that I can develop my own encyclopedia of symbols; that it is not necessary to understand the mythic archetypes of Jung's "collective unconscious" in precisely the same way he understood them.[7]

If I get stuck on what a symbol means, I will try to find the answer through meditation, simply quieting my mind, and visualization.

**9. Write what I think it is that God wants me to become aware of.**

Does what I learned from this dream increase my relationship with or understanding of God? How so? What is the lesson here? It's obvious to me now that I am being invited to explore what having FAITH means. I hope that in the process I can learn what God wants of me!

## 10. Save the dream and dreamwork paperwork.

I stapled the actual written dream on top of the dreamwork pages and dated the top. The dreamwork books emphasize keeping the original dream in case something in a future dream refers to a past dream. By reviewing the older dream's notes I might "see" something that I didn't notice or understand the first time I worked with the dream.

I'm excited about this new method—it worked well! *Meaning* came floating up, and I had those good *Aha!* feelings. Having a system was definitely the missing link when I tried dreamwork the first time around. I think I am ready to record—and hopefully decipher—whatever dreams the Divine has in store for me.

## February 22, 2007

Because I have been waking throughout the night to write the dreams down, then spending one to two hours each morning using the new system to work out their meanings, I am truly exhausted. Good thing I am retired. Otherwise, there would only be enough time for one or two dreams a week.

In the last few days, I have learned from dreams that I need to be patient and work diligently while keeping my journey private until I learn more. The social worker part of me wants to share what's happening, but I was cautioned not to. I had a dream that helped me let go of the heaviness I've been carrying around from my marriage to Tim; another helped me understand about foods I should and shouldn't eat; another taught me that inner growth has its own timetable—and that I have a tendency to want too much too soon.

This morning I had a headache, my knees and legs hurt and I could sense even before doing the dreamwork on last night's dream that I would be dealing with some uncomfortable issues. When I described my emotions in the dreamwork notes, I wrote "sadness," "despair," "isolation," and "feeling dejected." The dream is a long one that deals with the problems Tim and I had and why I chose him as a marriage partner. I am too drained to include all the details here, but in one part of the dream I am shown an unusual geometric symbol that seems significant:

> I THINK IT LOOKS SIMILAR TO A LARGE, SIMPLE HAIR COMB. OR, A LADDER WITH A SINGLE SOLID VERTICAL SECTION ON ONE SIDE. A MAN IN THE DREAM SAYS: "NO, TURN IT CURVED SO IT FORMS A CIRCULAR DESIGN. THE SEVEN COMPARTMENTS OR ROOMS AROUND THE OUTER SECTION ARE PLACES TO LEARN. THE CIRCLE IN THE CENTER REPRESENTS INNER BEING/HIGHER LEVEL."

The mandala-like symbol looked like this:

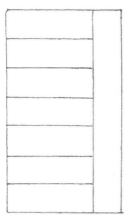

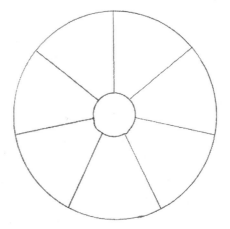

During the dreamwork, I wrote down these questions about the symbol: "Does it represent the theme of this night's dream or of all life? Why was it straight up and down at first, and why did the dream person have me change it into a circular design? Why seven compartments? Why does this symbol appear at the beginning of an emotionally challenging dream?" Working through the answers, I finally decided that part of what the circular symbol might mean is that I should not view individual life experiences in isolation; lessons to be learned in life are all related. In order for me to be whole—to have a strong relationship with myself, others, God, and the universe—I need to see those connections.

When I think about why the mandala-like symbol, with its feeling of significance, comes in this particularly weighty dream, I believe it came to assuage my fears; to let me know that this is a learning process. It also helped me reframe the dream's emotionally-laden issues so I can view them as opportunities for growth during this dreamwork process.

Overall the dreamwork today was emotionally challenging. Yet, afterward I felt free—no longer held fast by the effects of that dysfunctional marriage. I also felt able to accept responsibility for my contributions to its failure. I am starting to see that when it came to finding a partner, my ability to choose or function differently was tainted by my equally dysfunctional childhood.

I feel as if I'm not finished with these themes of my marriage and my childhood. Will I have more dreams on these subjects in the days to come? Am I ready?

৵৶

I've just come back from a massage where something amazing happened! As Lori began the massage, I asked her a rhetorical question: "Who are these helpers that appear in my dreams?" A few minutes later I had the first waking vision I have ever had. I was lying on the massage table, deeply relaxed, and *I SAW THE IMAGE OF*

A NATIVE AMERICAN MAN — HIS HEAD FROM A SIDE VIEW. I was surprised and puzzled. But then I remembered the question I had asked Lori. I took the vision as a gift from the Divine that has something to do with my question. But what? Why this particular image? Will I be given more information to figure this one out?

దొు

### February 23, 2007

Today I am not feeling nearly as beat-up, but this morning's dream feeds my confusion about the vision from yesterday:

> I AM PUTTING A TABLE TOGETHER THAT IS IN PIECES IN THE CLOSET. THE TABLE HAS A MONOPOLY BOARD BUILT INTO IT. I HEAR A VOICE IN THE DREAM SAY, "THE ARMY ISN'T GOING TO PUT TOGETHER THE PIECES OF YOUR TABLE THAT ARE YOUR MONOPOLY SET."

> WHEN I HEAR THAT THE ARMY WON'T HELP, I PLEAD NOT TO BE LEFT ALONE. I AM THEN SHOWN THE SAME INDIAN HEAD SYMBOL I HAD SEEN IN THE VISION, BUT THIS TIME HE IS ON A DARK FOREST-GREEN BACKGROUND WITH HIS HEAD ETCHED IN BRIGHT GOLDEN MOONLIGHT. I TAKE THIS AS AN AFFIRMATION THAT GOD KNOWS I UNDERSTOOD THE MESSAGE OF THE MONOPOLY BOARD, AND THAT HELP WILL BE THERE FOR ME.

Doing the dreamwork helped me figure out that the TABLE is a place where I eat, write, pay bills, do artwork, entertain—where life happens. I feel as if the dream is telling me that I cannot be helped if I insist on incorporating a *MONOPOLY GAME* into this *TABLE* of life; I am not to take over or monopolize; nor am I to view this work as a game. I have to ask for help. I have to understand that *I* am not in control, the Divine is!

What does the *INDIAN HEAD* symbol mean? In the dream, I feel as if it is an affirmation, but the fact that it has appeared twice now suggests that there is more meaning I have yet to understand.

⁊⊷⊰

After finishing the dreamwork today, I noticed the church bulletin that had been set on the table near my dream-paper pile on Ash Wednesday. When I picked it up and read Psalm 51, these three verses jumped out at me:

> *Indeed, you delight in truth deep within me, and would have me know wisdom deep within. Create in me a clean heart, O God, and renew a right spirit within me. Cast me not away from your presence, and take not your Holy Spirit from me.*[8]

Wow! Isn't this dreamwork journey about the very thing the psalm addresses—finding "truth deep within me"? Is this process a way to clean out my soul and "renew a right spirit within me"? Is God, in fact, delighted that I am on this journey? Is it really God who called me to this task, rather than my own wish? Did the psalmist experience a similar dream or fear—that God might take the Holy Spirit away, as I feared the *ARMY* would abandon me? Did the Divine just give me confirmation of the dream message in scripture?

Until today, I hadn't realized the seriousness and significance of what has been happening to me! Or, perhaps *I* haven't been as serious as I need to be about what has been happening. Each day I need to remember the ninth step in my new dreamwork plan: Ask the question, "What is it that God wants me to become aware of?"

I truly get it now. In order to grow my faith, I have to deal with and heal from the pain of past issues, learn to forgive, and therefore "create a clean heart." That is why these issues keep arising in my dreams! Which brings St. Paul's words to mind: *Through God all things work together for good if we ask for his forgiveness and love.*[9]

Trusting the process is what I am learning. The *MONOPOLY GAME* dream certainly makes it clear that I should not take this process and God too lightly. The *TABLE* can't stand—it doesn't have its legs, its support—without God as its foundation and guide.

❧

The dreams, the vision, the psalm . . . I feel as if I have reached some sort of turning point. I feel as if I am being led into new territory, that the dreams are preparing me for something . . .

*Toward dawn, when night and day touch*
*and for a moment intermingle and merge,*
*Henry's soul calmed down.*
*The images in his dream became*
*clearer and more coherent.*
**Christopher Bamford**[1]


*Make me to know your ways,*
*O Lord; teach me your paths.*
**Psalm 25:4**[2]


*Metaphor draws on images from the natural world,*
*from our senses,*
*and from the world of human social structures,*
*and yokes them to psychological and spiritual realities*
*in such a way that we're often left gasping;*
*we have no way to fully explain*
*a metaphor's power, it simply is.*
**Kathleen Norris**[3]

Chapter 4

# *The Voyage Begins*

Dreams: 1440,1440; *The Flying Ship; Labrador-Water Slide;*
*Wearing Out the Battery; Breathing Under Water;*
*The Medium Tilapia; The Monastery Gift*

## February 24, 2007

Nothing about my dreams last night seemed exceptional . . . until they were written down. The third one seemed different. It looked more like a literary piece, and I was anxious to do the dreamwork to figure it out. I have been wondering, though, if I will ever be sure that I am interpreting a dream correctly. What if I get it wrong? Will I be able to understand the things I am being taught?

Today's first dream segment:

> A SCHOOL TEACHER IS READING A LIST OF NUMBERS FOR ME TO WRITE DOWN, BUT SHE IS SAYING THEM TOO FAST. I ASK HER THREE TIMES TO REPEAT THEM, AND I STILL REMEMBER ONLY THE TOP TWO NUMBERS, WHICH ARE IDENTICAL: 1440, 1440

The teacher is Amy, who really does talk fast, but I wonder if because this dream occurred early in the night, it's just harder for me to retain information from the dream. Maybe the images just don't translate well from the dream source to the dreaming mind during the middle of the night. One of the times she reads, she displays the *LIST OF NUMBERS* in a way that doesn't make any sense to my dreaming or waking brain. The phrase "word-pictures" comes to mind, but I don't know if even that describes how she replaces the numbers with pictures.

When I woke up, I had no idea what *1440* meant, but my fuzzy brain thought it might refer to the dreaded 1040 tax form I have been working on lately. When I realized that I was missing documents needed to finish the 1040, I thought those documents were what the "missing" lower numbers of the teacher's sequence referred to! But, I had the number wrong: the dream number was *1440*, not 1040.

This afternoon, as I spent some more time working my way through the New Testament, I saw in the study notes for Revelation how numbers were given letters.[4] I decided to try it out on the mystery number from my dream: *1440*. It translated into the letters A, D, and D, but I found there was no translation for zero. At first I was confused, then amazed when I realized what it was about. Just yesterday, Bonnie told me that she dreamed about me. In *her* dream *I TELL HER THAT I HAVE ATTENTION DEFICIT DISORDER (ADD!), AND SHE SEES A RING WITH THE WORD "ABIDE" ON IT*. Of course! The "0" is the ring shape!

Even though I don't have ADD, my disorientation in this new world of dreamwork and metaphors has me feeling spacey! I don't know what to make of this except for the possibility that because the dream world is not a world of space/time or cause/effect, perhaps there are no boundaries between us as we dream.

After confusing *1440* with 1040, I made two other interpretation errors today—and felt stupid because of them. But, I was surprised to find that I still learned something despite the errors. Am I being taught that mistakes are part of the process? My stumbling around with the *1440* symbol might be a lesson that images can be multi-layered, with the possibility of multiple interpretations.

The second segment:

> I AM SUPPOSED TO TAKE A CHILD'S DESK HOME WITH ME. I FORGET. LINDA, A SCHOOL COUNSELOR, CALLS TO SEE IF I GOT IT. I SAY, "NO, I FORGOT IT." SHE SAYS SHE WILL GET IT.

Then:

> I AM IN A ROOM WITH A BIG HEAVY PIECE OF EQUIPMENT IN THE CORNER. I THINK THAT IF IT SLIDES TOWARD ME, I'LL BE PINNED. SO I'LL DO WHAT I HAVE TO DO, THEN CAREFULLY AND QUIETLY LEAVE THE ROOM. THE PIECE OF METAL MACHINERY LOOKS LIKE A HUGE, UPSIDE-DOWN ANCHOR. THERE IS A MOVABLE TABLE WITH TYPEWRITER ON IT. IT IS MOVED OUT TO THE CENTER OF THE ROOM, THEN, WHEN NOT BEING USED, I PUSH IT BACK TO ITS ALCOVE NESTLED BETWEEN CABINETS. IT MIGHT HAVE BEEN USED BY MARY.

Then this, *most* interesting segment:

> AN UNKNOWN VOICE SAYS: "I HAVE NEVER WORKED WITH SYMBOLS." I REPLY: "IT'S

HARDER TO WORK WITH PHYSICAL OBJECTS
THAN WITH WORDS." THEN I SEE AND WRITE
THE FOLLOWING: "NOW PEOPLE ARE COMING
BACK IN A BIG SHIP FLOATING ACROSS THE SKY.
THE MAN IN THE TOGA HAS BEEN LEISURELY
GOOFING OFF, BUT SEES THE BIG WOODEN
SHIP AND KNOWS HE HAS TO PREPARE AND
GET DOWN TO WORK. THEY ARE HERE." I SAY:
"IT'S EASY IF YOU FOLLOW SYSTEMATIC RULES.
WHEN YOU WORK WITH SYMBOLS YOU NEED A
DROP CLOTH."

After doing the dreamwork, the CHILD'S DESK suggests that I am at a basic level of learning, and the TYPEWRITER PULLED TO THE MIDDLE OF THE ROOM, THEN PUT BACK IN PLACE tells me that there is a time each day for doing my dreamwork, and a time to set it aside. I'm not sure what the connection to Mary is . . . she is well-read and quite literary; I wonder if she will teach me something? When the dreamwork steps were done, I couldn't elicit any clear meaning from the MACHINERY or HUGE ANCHOR symbol.

The written piece about the floating SHIP and the MAN IN THE TOGA has me confused. I've never written something like this in my dreams! I understand the basic information about the systematic rules and working with symbols, but I don't find this particular written symbol EASY.

Despite my confusion, one message stands out overall: It's okay to make mistakes—"WHEN YOU WORK WITH SYMBOLS YOU NEED A DROP CLOTH." I feel comforted by that, as well as comforted to see that not only am I being taught how to heal myself and how to grow my faith, but I'm also being given lessons about how to do dreamwork!

## February 25, 2007

Last night I dreamed:

*AGAIN I SEE NUMBERS ONE AFTER ANOTHER THAT I CAN'T REMEMBER. I SLIDE DOWN A STEEP SLIDE, SKIDDING ACROSS THE GROUND A LONG WAY ON GRAVEL, SAYING, "WE'VE GOT TO FIX THIS!" THEN I AM JUMPING WITH A LABRADOR RETRIEVER OFF A 100-FOOT CLIFF INTO WATER, BUT THE DOG AND I ARE MADE TO GO BACK. I WONDER IF WE HAVE DONE SOMETHING WRONG.*

Immediately following, I woke up with the beginning of a migraine. Too tired to get up and do anything about it, I rolled onto my side and the strangest thing happened: My head felt dizzy and there was a rushing sound in my right ear—my blood pulsing. Then the sound stopped. I wondered if I was having a stroke. Instead, I lay there a minute until I realized my headache was gone! After a few minutes, I fell back to sleep and dreamed:

*I AM RUNNING SIXTY MILES AN HOUR DOWN A FLIGHT OF WOODEN STAIRS AND SOMETHING FLIES OUT OF MY PURSE, FALLS TO THE FLOOR BELOW, AND ROLLS OVER TO A WOMAN NAMED CHLOE, WHO WORKS IN THIS AREA. I SAY, "I BET THIS HAPPENS A LOT!" SHE SMILES AND SAYS, "NOT REALLY," AND HANDS IT BACK TO ME. SHE ALERTS ME TO THE OBJECT, WHICH I SEE IS A BATTERY AND THAT IT HAS BEEN DAMAGED AND IS LEAKING. I LAY THE CONTENTS OF THE INSIDE POCKET OF MY PURSE ON THE*

COUNTER AND REALIZE THAT THE PALM OF MY
HAND BURNS FROM TINY PINPRICKS OF ACID.
I TELL SOMEONE WITH ME THAT I AM LUCKY
I FOUND THIS OUT! I BUNDLE THE OBJECTS UP
AND GIVE THEM TO CHLOE, WHO IS HOLDING
HER HANDS OUT TO RECEIVE THEM. AMONG
THE ITEMS IS A PAIR OF SUN VISORS/GLASSES. I
LATER HEAR A VOICE SAY: "WHEN YOU LEARN
TO NAVIGATE, IT'S A LOT EASIER!"

From doing the dreamwork steps, I figured out that these dreams share a central message: I need to quit trying to remember my dreams all night long or I will wear myself out (like the BATTERY). Maybe the dream process has been hindered by continually waking up to record dreams . . .

Dreamwork books say that the most significant dream of the night is the one toward morning[5] and I'm finding that my most complete and instructive dreams occur between 5 and 7 a.m. If I do have an important coherent dream earlier in the night, I think I'm becoming aware enough that I will be able to recognize it.

Although it will be hard for me to not wake up and record dreams, I know I had better listen to the message if I want to learn what the Holy Spirit is teaching. The voices and dream figures are kind, helpful, and patient with me, as though I am a child. Actually . . . I *feel* like a child.

I am definitely on a journey—I know it. My sense of intrigue and excitement is building.

శి∞ఈ

## February 26, 2007

I woke up in the middle of the night filled with joy! In my dream I was learning how to breathe under water—what a feeling!

> *BREATHING UNDER WATER IS KIND OF HARD TO GET THE HANG OF BECAUSE IT'S THE OPPOSITE OF WHAT I'M USED TO DOING. BUT I SEE LOTS OF PEOPLE LEARNING, AND IT IS FUN SWIMMING UNDER WATER WITHOUT HAVING TO GO UP FOR AIR.*

I wonder if SWIMMING UNDER WATER is a metaphor for dreaming in the unconscious realm . . . Or, like when I had the TINK dream, is it simply because I sometimes stop breathing while I'm sleeping? Maybe it's a breathing lesson. If my breathing is uninterrupted, I *will* be more likely to sleep and dream . . .

The same night that I dreamed of the teacher reciting the numbers and of the FLYING SHIP, there was a tiny dream segment I didn't write down here because it didn't seem significant at the time. In the segment, I am outside a RESTAURANT, but I don't know what I want so I leave without going in. This morning, I am back at that same restaurant, but now I am inside sitting down:

> *"I'LL TAKE THAT FISH NOW, PLEASE," I SAY. "THE TILAPIA?" SAYS THE WAITER. "YES," I SAY. "DO YOU WANT IT MEDIUM OR WELL DONE?" HE ASKS. "IS IT SAFE TO EAT IT MEDIUM?" I REPLY. "YES," HE SAYS. "I'LL TAKE IT MEDIUM," I RESPOND.*

### I HEAR A MAN'S VOICE SAY, "STEP UP TO THE HOLY GRILL!"

Yet another food symbol! Is the Holy Spirit giving me lessons in healthy eating? I'll have to pay attention to see if this is a recurring theme.

Looking for both literal and symbolic interpretations of the TILAPIA, I see it may be about eating nutritious food; or it could represent Jesus and my Christian beliefs. I wonder why I try it MEDIUM—I always eat fish WELL DONE.

Brainstorming on the word MEDIUM I came up with: adventurous, not finished, not dry, or a method used to create, like an art medium. WELL DONE might mean the accepted version of Christ, or dry, tough, inflexible, rubbery, hard to chew and swallow. When I was finished I started to feel uncomfortable. For the past three years I have reconnected with my solid Christian roots. Am I being asked to stretch a little? Will I lose something important I love and have rediscovered? Just when I'm finally starting to understand traditional mainstream Christianity, am I being nudged toward looking at my faith in a more adventurous way?

What does "STEP UP TO THE HOLY GRILL" mean? I tried word play and came up with HOLY—something spiritual; STEP UP to the plate, dinner plate, baseball plate, get ready to play ball, to enter into the game, the spirit of the game, into the arena of debate—debate about the GRILL, about the sacred fire, Holy Grail, or history of Jesus? Of Christianity?

My upcoming visit with Susan (our diaconal minister) has been on my mind. She recently went to a presentation by Marcus Borg and John Dominic Crossan—the more non-traditional Bible scholars. Is this dream about that? Will she share something with me that will make me look at my Christian faith differently? Am I being encouraged to be open-minded?

আ৺

Some time was spent today reviewing the dreams from the past few weeks, and I think I'm starting to understand more about specifics within the dreams:

1. From studying the dreamwork books, I know to look at all dream elements and symbols as parts of myself. There are often three main characters in my dreams: my dreamself, a younger dream character, and a wiser, spiritual character who usually offers some instruction in the dream. In some dreams the older character seems to lead the dream journey.

2. The age of my dreamself or a dream character may signal what the focus of the dream is about: the metaphorical representation of a person of that age, something that occurred or relates to when I was that age, or something that is characteristic of a person of that age. Metaphorically, a baby might represent new knowledge, beginning a project, or new life. A baby might also represent a responsibility that needs to be addressed, or an inner need that requires attention.

3. Shadowy or dark characters represent something about me that I need to become aware of. In a dream from the other night I saw an older dark

couple. After doing the dreamwork, I realized they represented the problem I was having (but ignoring) with Adrian. I knew then that we had to talk about it before it affected my attitude and behavior toward him.

4. Direction is important.A dream character's physical placement in relation to my dreamself, as well as the direction in which we move, are helpful to interpreting information in a dream. If the character, symbol, or movement is to the *right*, it indicates something that refers to my *outer, physical* life. If it is on the *left*, it refers to my *spiritual life*, or *inner, unconscious mind*. Moving *up* indicates moving to the *outer conscious* level, or to a *higher spiritual* level. Which one it is becomes apparent after doing the dreamwork. *Down* is a movement to a deeper *unconscious* level, as in the WEARING OUT THE BATTERY dream, when I was running *down* the steps. But, if the previous activity in the dream was at a higher level of learning, *down* might be to the *outer conscious* level.

If I had known this two years ago, I wouldn't have missed a key piece of information in this dream:

> I WALKED DOWN THE CORRIDOR OF A MONASTERY. THERE WAS A PACKAGE ON THE FLOOR TO MY RIGHT UNDER A WINDOW. I REACHED FOR THE PACKAGE AND AS I PICKED IT UP, I HEARD THE WORDS, "A CHANT, A CHANT, TO CONNECT WITH GOD."

Upon my waking, I heard the "Come Holy Spirit" prayer in my head: *"Come Holy Spirit, Fill the hearts of Thy faithful; enkindle in them the fire of Thy love. Send forth Your spirit that they shall be created, and Thou shall renew the face of the earth."* I remember saying it often when I was little.

Originally I thought the PACKAGE was simply the gift of the prayer, until a few days later, while on a retreat at Grailville. After breakfast at the retreat house, I was trying to find a picture of a dove to draw—something Celtic if it could be found. In the bookstore, there was a picture of a dove in a large Celtic print by a local artist. The artist was Cindy Matyi, the print was entitled "Calling the Spirit," and on the back of the print was the prayer, "Come Holy Spirit"![6]

That was such an amazing moment. Now when I think of it I realize that the PACKAGE referred to a gift in the future because it was ON MY RIGHT and UNDER A WINDOW, which indicated that it might manifest in my physical world. When I think of how both the PACKAGE in the dream and the print in outer life were found in spiritual places (a MONASTERY and a retreat center), I am awed.

I am feeling much better about the dreamwork process and know that I am being guided on this journey. But, I'm worried that this journey may require me to be mentally and spiritually open to new adventures and learning—I'm not sure about trying that TILAPIA!

## Lessons I am Learning about Dreamwork

I am sure that I am not only embarking on an exciting spiritual journey, but that I am also being taught how to do dreamwork in the process. To keep it all straight, I am going to list the "lessons" as they come.

**Lesson #1**

**Mistakes.** Don't worry about making mistakes. Misinterpretations may happen for a reason.

**Lesson #2**

**Morning Dreams.** The last dream of the night, the one near dawn, is usually the most coherent, complete, and helpful. It is the culmination, the summary, of what my unconscious mind has been working on all night with the help of the Holy Spirit. It is more important to rest than it is to wake up to record middle-of-the-night dreams.

**Lesson #3**

**Messages.** Each night's dream contains a message. The message may pertain to the upcoming day or possibly to a situation that will occur in the future. Sometimes, the message may clarify or build on something from the past. Reviewing the morning's dream and dreamwork after living the day can help understand the message and a possible theme that may be emerging.

**Lesson #4**

**Dreamselves and Movement.** Dreams often contain three main characters: the learner or dreamself; an older, wiser spiritual self; and a younger self. The placement of the characters and the directions in which they move is significant. Moving up or down stairs or hills represents moving to "higher learning" or "down into the unconscious." The movements to the right, or objects on the right (of my dreamself), tend to signify something in the outer physical world. Movements to the left, or objects on the left, tend to signify the inner spiritual world.

# PART II

# FORGIVENESS

*Our senses require healing and rehabilitation so that
they are adequate for receiving and responding to
visitations and appearances of Spirit,
God's Holy Spirit . . .*
**Eugene H. Peterson[1]**

*For by grace you have been saved through faith,
and this is not your own doing;
it is the gift of God—not the result of works
so that no one may boast.
For we are what he has made us,
created in Christ Jesus for good works,
which God prepared beforehand to be our way of life.*
**Ephesians 2:8-10[2]**

*When we are open we find that the depths of ourselves
are revealed to us.
God presents us with ourselves, and then,
as we work with Him to understand and grow,
He draws us closer to Himself.*
**Morton Kelsey[3]**

Chapter 5

# Messy, Stinky Things

Dreams: *The Treadmill; The Poopy Toddler*

## February 28, 2007

Recording the details of yesterday morning's dream tires me so, but I realize now that it was showing me my problematic, childish behavior of turning a cold shoulder and withdrawing from a relationship when I get upset.

This morning's dream seems to build on that one by giving me another image that shows a problem with my personality.

In the dream I bet that I know how much a man in the dream weighs compared to me, and I will pay the COST of the difference if I am wrong.

WE GET ON THE SCALE TO SEE WHAT WE EACH WEIGH. AS I STAND ON IT, THE SCALE TURNS INTO A WALKING MACHINE: A TREADMILL. I WALK AND WALK, AND FINALLY, RUN. I NOTICE THAT THE HANDLES BECOME SEPARATED FROM THE WALKWAY, AND AS I WALK, THE WALKWAY PART STARTS TO SLIDE BEHIND ME—OUT FROM UNDER MY FEET. I TURN IT IN A DIFFERENT DIRECTION—I CANNOT SAY WHICH—AND IT STILL HAPPENS, WHETHER I AM ON A HILL OR NOT.

The TREADMILL is a fascinating symbol! The obvious literal meaning is that I need to resume my outdoor walks even though it's cold and I don't want to.

Symbols:

1) On the TREADMILL, I get nowhere. I am doing an action or activity over and over the same old way. I can walk or run and still accomplish nothing.

2) Worse . . . the HANDLE comes away from the frame. I am holding onto something that is not connected. The MACHINE is me and I can't work without connection, without being whole. One part can't work without all the parts working together—whether I am talking about myself, my family, or my church community.

3) My guessing and betting on knowing a sure thing gets me into trouble. Even when I turn the TREADMILL in a DIFFERENT DIRECTION, put myself in a new situation, the TREADMILL parts are still disconnected.

4) The disconnect is between my inner knowing and my outer behavior. I can run on the TREADMILL all I want—stay busy, exercise, or throw myself into my job. If I do not seek help with the underlying behavior or problem, I can't resolve anything, and I can't accomplish anything spiritual. I am running in place, treading water, or off base. I understand the dream's message: when I

have a know-it-all attitude, I can't learn or progress. As long as there is a disconnect between my actions and my inner spiritual guidance, I cannot grow. In biblical terms, sinning causes a separation from God.

*Aha!* This dream is about that part of my personality that prejudges others, the know-it-all who sizes someone up and puts them in a box, labels them, and decides how to respond—not based on their being a child of God but on a reflection of what I dislike within myself or what is different from myself. I know this is mostly an unconscious process. It is what has caused me to feel fearful of unfamiliar people or people of different races whom I perceive as different from me. It is the same thing that leads to hatred and wars!

All of this from an image of a treadmill? How does so much meaning come bubbling up from this dreamwork? It must come from the Holy Spirit, because it certainly isn't coming from me. I need to remember to do the work itself, to follow the method and to keep myself centered on this journey with God. The meaning itself comes *to* me, not *from* me. It is coming to me as I work with these dream symbols, these valuable images, these *gifts*.

I am beginning to see that when the dream content is more emotionally charged or more difficult because it addresses issues I have trouble facing head-on, the problem behavior appears in a dream character that doesn't feel like my dreaming self at first. Also, this corrective type of dream seems to soften the emotional impact of what I am being taught by leaving the matter open-ended for me to figure out.

After I dreamed of the TREADMILL, I dreamed:

*I PICK UP A TODDLER AND HE IS POOPY. THERE IS GREEN POOP ALL THE WAY DOWN THE STEPS WHERE HE HAS COME FROM. AS I HOLD HIM, I KNOW I WILL CLEAN HIM UP.*

This dream is open-ended—and uncomfortable! Similar images of the BABY/TODDLER and POOP have occured in other dreams. Symbolically, GREEN is the color of growth, healing, newness or rawness, or needing to be finished or ripened. The BABY represents my beginning growth, which can be messy; and that growth comes from dealing with "messy, stinky things" that I'd rather not look at, smell, touch, or get close to!

The dream of Mom on January 26th was also open-ended. When she says, "IT'S A MATTER OF FAITH," and the dream ends with my dreamself's statement, "BUT . . . I BELIEVE"—a sort of childlike whine trying to convince her that I have it together—the dream seems to be questioning, "But, Candy . . . do you really? Is saying, 'I believe in God' all there is to faith?" No! But I can't just leave it there. I must rise to the challenge to find out what having faith really entails. What is it I believe? Do I even know anything about God or God's promises? Or how to have a closer relationship with the Divine?

If I am going to commit to doing dreamwork, to accept the challenge or task put before me, I must respond *(ACT!)* to Mom's thought-provoking statement.

❧

The dreams are starting to address my shadow places, my dark (unconscious) places. When I first started this crash course in dreamwork, I wanted to learn about how to have a closer relationship with God. What I didn't know is that this dream process isn't just fun stuff about faith and dream techniques. Cleaning me up now seems to be high on my dream world's agenda. It must be that, in order to understand God better, I have to also understand myself better! Is this a realization of the idea of Baptism: immersion in the cleansing flow of meaning from within?

I am fascinated when the Divine gives me dreams that enable me to look at what should be painful memories, but they are often done in a creative and sometimes comical way—and always for healing, not for condemnation. Knowing that I am not setting the agenda each night makes it exciting. I can only wonder what will come next, and trust!

In THE TREADMILL dream, the COST of being wrong (the bet) is so exorbitant that I can never pay. In some dreams, as in life, I am left with only one solution: ask for forgiveness and throw myself on the mercy of God. When I act grievously, and get myself too deep over my head, only God's grace and mercy can rescue me!

At this point, I know I want to stay connected to my inner self and the Divine. I want to continue with this intriguing dreamwork and to continue reading the Bible to see how it interweaves with my dreams. I understand why Martin Luther said, "We are all beggars." I can't understand problematic behaviors and destructive patterns in myself without the Holy Spirit's help. Divine intervention is needed in overcoming them. This work with dreams and their symbols is getting me there.

*Lessons I am Learning about Dreamwork*

**Lesson #5**

**Symbols.** I can work with a dream symbol to elicit many meanings: even *parts* of the symbol may be significant.

**Lesson #6**

**Open-ended Dreams.** Many dreams are left open-ended, unanswered, hanging in mid-air, with my dreamself feeling sad or confused. The dream seems to want me to think through and arrive at not only some possible ideas but some *action*. The dream has a message for me to think about, similar to Christ's parables.

In repenting of sin we are not turning away in order to
be someone else but returning to our true selves,
made in the loveliness
and goodness of the image of God.
**J. Philip Newell**[1]

Peter said to them, "Repent, and be baptized every one
of you in the name of Jesus Christ so that your sins may
be forgiven and you will receive the gift of
the Holy Spirit."
**Acts 2:38**[2]

God works with us as we are and not as we should be
or think we should be.
God deals with us where we are
and not where we would like to be.
**Eugene H. Peterson**[3]

If you get the inside right, the outside will fall into
place. Primary reality is within,
secondary reality without.
**Eckhart Tolle**[4]

Chapter 6

# A Bathroom Breakthrough

Dream: *The White Truck; The Geisha*

## March 1, 2007

This morning's dream is the most complex dream of any to date. As I write it down, it seems disjointed, with eight scenes that bounce back and forth between three settings. The dreamwork hasn't been done yet, but I can see that the theme of my past problem-causing behaviors continues:

> I AM AT A SCHOOL WHERE I HAVE BEEN A SUBSTITUTE TEACHER. A DETECTIVE HAS ME SITTING IN A CAR, WATCHING, TO POINT OUT A YOUNG BLOND STUDENT WHO ALWAYS MAKES EXCUSES, CLAIMING THAT SHE DOESN'T DO WRONG THINGS. WE SLIDE DOWN IN THE CAR SO WE WON'T BE SEEN RIGHT AWAY. WE PULL IN THE DRIVEWAY AND A WHITE TRUCK IS BLOCKING THE WAY, CROSSWISE IN FRONT OF US, FACING TO THE RIGHT.

In a moving car I am on some kind of discovery journey. We pull in a DRIVEWAY near a SCHOOL (place of learning). I am supposed to be watching what a YOUNG BLOND STUDENT (a younger me) is up to. Two dream symbols are there to assist: a DETECTIVE, a dream authority from the unconscious, to help me investigate something, and a WHITE (holy/spiritual) TRUCK blocking my path. The WHITE TRUCK is blocking me physically, but it could also imply that I am being stopped from proceeding with my journey until I figure out what's here for me to learn from and about that young me.

*Aha!* This content is of the utmost importance. It is the *Holy Spirit* who is doing the blocking. It's clear I am not going anywhere until I glean the wisdom from this dream.

Two of the two dream symbols (DETECTIVE, TRUCK) are viewed as masculine images. I also associate two of the symbolic images—HAS ME SITTING IN A CAR and WE SLIDE DOWN IN THE CAR SO WE WON'T BE SEEN—with illicit sexual behavior. This dream has to do with unexamined sexual issues, such as the sexual fantasies of other men during those lonely twenty-seven years of my marriage

Sexual fantasies are symbols and I am not alone in experiencing them. They are a symbolic activity common in human life. On the conscious side, I know sexual fantasies are seldom helpful. They cause separation and isolation and may lead to problematic behaviors. But if I look at these symbols from the side of the unconscious, they can be seen as an expression of my need to be loved and feel alive. In an unconscious way, they are born out of an attempt to become whole.

In the second scene:

> MOM AND DAD HAVE BOUGHT A HOUSE IN
> LOVELAND, ALTHOUGH I'M NOT SURE WHY. IT'S
> A BIT FAR FROM THEIR FAMILY AND CHURCH.

MOM TELLS ME OF THIS MOVE, AND I AM VERY SURPRISED.

My view of LOVELAND is that place where I, they, and so many, expect to live out the rest of our married lives. But the particular idea of LOVELAND in this dream is not the ideal. The love in this house is off the mark, FAR FROM THEIR FAMILY AND CHURCH.

They so believed in healthy committed love, but that was thwarted by their financial, marital, and alcohol problems. Dad's drinking and Mom's resulting emotional distance took their toll. Was it inevitable that my first marriage followed similar patterns and that my behavior, and his, over the years caused irreparable damage?

Back at the school in the dream:

TWO LITTLE GIRLS, SISTERS, ARE VERY BORED. THEY WANT ME TO DO THINGS WITH THEM. WE ARE AT SCHOOL, BUT NOW I AM NOT ACTING AS A TEACHER. I CONTEMPLATE TAKING THEM TO A MOVIE BUT I'M NOT SURE THERE IS ONE SUITABLE FOR KIDS.

This is about how Judy and I were bored and somewhat on our own in childhood because of Mom and Dad's emotional distance. Metaphorically, maybe the outer child that I was and the inner, soul child that still retains a memory of that time, want help. We are at SCHOOL . . . a place of learning. These TWO LITTLE GIRLS (twin symbols) want me to do something. I see that exploring the problems hinted at in this dream entails looking at adult themes.

Fourth scene:

> I AM IN THE SCHOOL BATHROOM. IT IS A BIG
> ROOM. A FAMILIAR MAN IS IN THERE TOO. I AM
> EMBARRASSED BECAUSE I CAN'T SEEM TO WIPE
> POOP OFF ADEQUATELY. IT IS STICKY, AND I USE
> A LOT OF TOILET PAPER. TWO OTHER WOMEN
> WALK BY AND I AM EMBARRASSED THAT THEY
> SEE THE MESS IN THE TOILET.

This is another dream trying to get me to look at undesirable behavior and to acknowledge how uncomfortable I am both in looking at it and in sharing it! Toilets seem to be the perfect image for the unconscious working out old inner stuff—the memories that haunt or cause guilt, the baggage that gets in the way of loving and feeling loved by God.

❧

I've done the dreamwork and realize that, in this dream, POOP is a symbol for embarrassing issues—memories that have stuck to me, of which I haven't been able to rid myself. I recognize the MAN in the bathroom—we knew each other a long time ago. He always liked to brainstorm and work through problems. I realize the dreamwork is doing just that.

Part of the fifth scene:

> I DRIVE PAST A PRETTY PARK OUTSIDE THE
> SCHOOL. A BOY AND GIRL ARE WITH ME, AS
> WELL AS A MAN. THE CHILDREN WANT TO
> PLAY IN THE PARK, BUT I THINK THEY MAY
> BE OVERDRESSED.

The BOY AND GIRL (youthful masculine and feminine aspects of my soul) want to play, to be social, and to fit in with friends. But I also sense that there is still work to do. I can't play if I am OVERDRESSED. Metaphorically, my OVERDRESSED clothes are hiding who I really am! I am presenting myself as holier or loftier than I really am. I know my past and my sins. At the literal level, I feel as if I have a false face, hiding the lies of who I have been and what I have done. Realizing that I do not need to announce my former sins to my friends, but that I do need to release myself from the old baggage that haunts me still, gives me a greater sense of freedom. However, I am still not fully willing to be out in the world as a less than completely virtuous person.

The sixth scene:

> BACK IN THE SCHOOL, THINGS ARE DISAPPEARING. ARE THEY BEING STOLEN? THE SCHOOL OFFICIALS ARE TRYING TO FIGURE OUT WHO IS DOING IT. THEY SUSPECT THE YOUNG BLOND STUDENT WHO HAS GIVEN ME THE SAME EXCUSE FOR THE LAST THREE OR FOUR YEARS. I TELL THIS TO THE DETECTIVE. IT HAS BEEN INFREQUENT THAT I SUBSTITUTE TEACH, AND NOT MUCH AT ALL IN THE LAST YEAR AND A HALF.

Back in the SCHOOL, the place of higher learning, THINGS ARE DISAPPEARING. My first reaction was to think that the STUDENT (me) was guilty of stealing. But now I don't think so. I believe that what is disappearing is the baggage from my past.

Even when my faith was renewed three years ago and felt as if I had been forgiven, I still never understood my youthful behaviors or where they came from. When I say I haven't SUBSTITUTE TAUGHT much it means that these behaviors weren't looked at enough, at least not seriously enough. The dream is telling me there is a need to deal with these past issues, this shadow part of me!

The seventh scene:

> IN THE SCHOOL BATHROOM, I GRUNT TO GO. I DECIDE TO IGNORE THE MAN THAT IS STILL IN THERE AND JUST GET IT OUT. I ONLY HAVE A LITTLE LEFT TO DO. HE STANDS BY THE DOOR TO MY RIGHT. I AM NOT SURE IF HE IS SMILING OR SMIRKING.

Yes! Out went the poop that has had me plugged up. Even though I could take this literally and relate it to my worsening constipation problem, my study of dreams revealed that bowel-movement images are used metaphorically for things that keep us blocked. I truly feel this is what the dream is about. The same familiar man is still in the bathroom. How am I like him? When I knew him he was always fearful about what other people thought of him. How do I identify with him? I have been afraid of what others, especially those loved ones near and dear to me, would think of my past actions. But I think my dreamself is saying, "Oh the heck with it, I'm getting this sticky, messy stuff out once and for all!" And whether he is smiling or smirking . . . I don't care—I want to be rid of this stuff!

The eighth and final scene:

WE DROVE BY THAT PRETTY PARK AND SLOWED
DOWN TO LOOK AT IT. AT FIRST I DIDN'T SEE
MUCH OF IT, AND I THOUGHT IT WAS VERY
SMALL. THEN, BECAUSE I WANTED TO SEE IT,
BECAUSE OF MY GAZING AT IT, THE IMAGE
OPENED UP MORE CLEARLY INTO A MUCH
LARGER PARK WITH BEAUTIFUL GREEN GRASS
AND TREES LINING IT. IT GREW FROM A SMALL
PLOT INTO A CITY PARK AN ENTIRE BLOCK
LONG. THE PARENTS WOULD APPROVE OF THE
KIDS PLAYING HERE.

One explanation for the PARK could be that it is a place
of rest and relaxation. I want to be there—a respite from
these inner and outer problems. It may also be symbolic of
my life: At first, my sight reveals only a small plot, a small
section of my past, and not the whole picture. But because
my deep inner self desires the truth, the helpers guide me
into gazing at the problems that cause me to be stuck, and
this allows me to see the much larger PARK and a more
expansive view of my life opens up! I feel as if they are
showing me there is a great deal more to me than the few
things I have done wrong.

It's amazing how both the guilt learned as a child when
I had done something wrong, and the *don't tell anyone*
attitude that kept inner conflicts locked inside throughout
my life have left a weight on my soul that my conventional
renewal of faith could not remove!

Assuredly, this dream is a gift from the Holy Spirit
of forgiveness—complete forgiveness that comes with
understanding the behavior that is forgiven.

Now that this unconscious understanding has been brought to my consciousness, old painful memories are viewed in a kinder and gentler manner. Wow! This new insight is a gift—a gift in addition to the knowledge and certainty that I have the Divine's forgiveness. Now I can let go of the guilt, shame, and embarrassment—and the hidden lies as well.

☙❧

Something more has happened—a beautiful comment from the dream world on this very dreamwork that's been done today. While I was doing the dreamwork, a real storm was crashing and banging outside the window. I lay down to rest as the storm subsided and the rain stopped. I nodded off and dreamed:

> I SEE A BEAUTIFUL GEISHA LIFT HER LOVELY
> HEAD FROM THE PILLOW. SHE HAS RED LIPS
> AND SHE IS LOOKING TO MY LEFT (INNER)
> AS IF LISTENING. SHE KNOWS THE STORM IS
> FINALLY GONE.

What a beautiful image of this work! I am learning that my life is much bigger than just what is apparent at the outer conscious level. It is becoming ever more clear to me that the inner world is just as real as the outer world.

☙❧

I'm intrigued by the WHITE CAR, the POOPY TODDLER, and the PARK in this morning's dream. My desire is to know more about them, and I am still not sure that my understanding is correct. I suspect the images have layers of meaning. As is evident in the WHITE TRUCK dream, they don't always spell out the issues clearly. I am going to ask the Holy Spirit for guidance in interpreting these images.

I used to think that much of the night's unintelligible gibberish was the bits and pieces of my day carried into my subconscious mind at night, often for no real purpose. Now I am realizing that the Holy Spirit guides my unconscious by using the content and images of the prior day, combining them with the conflicts and problem issues with which I am struggling, and works this mix to give me an incredibly rich and creative dream that speaks to me and gives me guidance about those issues. This inner process works toward wholeness and motivates behaviors and choices, often and most times without conscious awareness. I am in awe of how looked after I am. The Bible is filled with dreams and visions that guided God's children. I am learning that, thousands of years later, even I can access this same wisdom!

## *Lessons I am Learning about Dreamwork*

### Lesson #7

**Literal vs. Symbolic.** It helps to view a symbol, image, behavior, or situation from a literal point of view, then to examine it from a symbolic/metaphorical view. One view may or may not be more helpful than the other. It seems that the meanings are imbedded in the symbols; they are implicit, not explicit. Also, when the symbol is a person it is important to ask the questions, "How am I like him/her? How do I identify with him/her?"

# PART III

# UNDERSTANDING

*They might also receive a message concerning
their diets.
They would be encouraged to eat some foods,
or warned against eating other kinds of foods.*
**Vine Deloria Jr.[1]**

*To each is given the manifestation of the Spirit
for the common good.*
**1 Corinthians 12:7[2]**

*. . . if you know and have been affected by your
dreams, you will feel in yourself a thread of meaning
and purpose that is a part of something much bigger
than yourself. This is the faith that lives in me.
If this faith corresponds to reality then our dreams,
which are the Voice of the living God within,
are also connected to the transcendent God
who is behind all of the universe.*
**John Sanford[3]**

Chapter 7

# *Working with Symbols*

Dreams: *Pick Ten; Free Beef*

**March 2, 2007**

At the Spiritual Gifts class last night, Susan saw that every one of the ten of us had a chance to participate. But at the close of the evening I worried that perhaps the earnest student in me had talked too much—took too much of the group's time . . .

This morning I dreamed:

> I AM TOLD TO PICK 10 ITEMS. I DON'T DO VERY WELL—ABOUT 8 OF THEM ARE POKER CHIPS OR BUTTONS. "NO—PICK OTHER SMALL OBJECTS," SAYS A VOICE, "LIKE A SQUARE CUBE OF BREAD, AN OLD SAM COOKE RECORD, A BLOCK OF WOOD—THINGS WITH SOME KIND OF MEANING."

I am excited and I suspect this dream is leading me to learn more about interpreting symbols:

> **10** = a perfect number, complete, a decade, the top as in the top on a scale of one to ten; I have just had 10 dreams about the theme of Forgiveness; we had 10 people at the

Spiritual Gifts class last night. According to *The Herder Dictionary of Symbols*, ten is "a holy number, a return to unity on a higher level and of the circle closing on itself."[4]

**Poker Chips** = gambling pieces, playing/ gambling at life instead of using symbolic wisdom to guide me; fake money, fake riches. Poker could mean to prod, to stir up. Chip could mean cow chip used for fires; to stir up the fire.

**Button** = inconsequential; "button, button, who's got the button?" — a game; inexpensive, of not much value, no meaning or feeling. I have no attachment to buttons, so choosing this item is not a good choice since I am supposed to be choosing something with meaning. Yet, buttons hold things together; they fasten two pieces so they don't come apart; they keep things in place.

I am starting to see from this word play that even simple items used as symbols have a *positive* and a *negative* aspect to them.

The bread cube looked like it was whole wheat with raisins . . .

**Bread cube** = nourishment, recipe/cooking; literally — feeding people; figuratively — sharing nourishment/information that is helpful; not just plain old white bread but healthy whole wheat with raisins; more substantial. Could this symbol mean the gifts of hospitality and service? In my dream it appeared dry. Why is it stale? Because I'm not using this gift—not having friends over for dinner? Should I be volunteering at a soup kitchen? Or literally, not eating healthy breads, leaving them to go stale while making other, less healthy, selections? Bread is the symbol of life, sustenance, of Christ's body, spiritual sustenance.

**Old Sam Cooke record** = The only Sam Cooke song I remember is "Cupid," that record from when I was fifteen about falling in love. This symbol is about music, a good singing voice, and a powerful message at an impressionable age. As an object, the black plastic record is of no value in and of itself, but what it produces—what comes from it— is powerful, reaches millions, and influences a generation of kids. What is the gift? Does it have something to do with my singing in the church choir? Could it be that this symbol is speaking of the gift of vocal music?

**Block of wood** = hard, grown from the earth; to get a *block* of wood means it is man-made, a human construct. The piece of wood, like the black plastic record, is of no worth in and of itself, but it produces objects/constructs that are important. Constructs, construction— wood is used to build, i.e. ships, stairs, tables. Wooden symbols are something to be built on, something created. Christ was a carpenter; he built objects/constructs for people to continue building on.

Looking at these word associations, I see that certain ones stand out and that some symbols can have both a positive and a negative aspect. They can mirror the negative traits within me as well as the positive—even show me my spiritual gifts . . .

> The positive aspect of the bread symbol is nourishment; the negative aspect, since it is stale, might be that what it represents is not being utilized.

> The negative aspect of the wood is that it can be hard, which makes me think of the words "blockhead" and "dense," not able to catch on; the positive aspect is that wood is used as construction material. It is rough or smooth, of the earth, and it feeds fires.

In my second dream:

> EARLIER I GOT PACKS OF MEAT AT A FREE STORE. I HAD BEEN TOLD TO TAKE SOME, AND I HAD PUT A COUPLE OF PACKS ON THE COUNTER. THEN, A SHORT TIME LATER, I TOOK A COUPLE MORE. THE ATTENDANT SAID I WAS TAKING TOO MUCH—MORE THAN MY SHARE. IT WAS BEEF. I PUT SOME PACKS BACK AND ONLY TOOK TWO. IN MY LEFT EAR I HEARD SOMEONE TAKING A BITE OF AN APPLE.

Literally I see that the dream is reminding me that in order to control my high cholesterol, my consumption of BEEF should only be twice a week (I'll miss my steaks). Symbolically, it is answering my concern about taking up too much of the group's time last night. Is it helping me ask the question, "How am I not allowing others to have their fair share?"

Another symbolic version of the MEAT is that it could be about the spiritual gift of Giving (time/talent/money). How do I know when giving is enough or not enough? The positive aspect of this version of the MEAT symbol is that it is a FREE gift, freely given. The negative side of either version is that giving too much is unhealthy, exhausting, or may deprive others of sharing and participating.

As I'm sitting on the couch right now doing this dreamwork, I just noticed a very large truck with its engine running right outside the front window. It is blocking the entire road.

Could this be an outer manifestation of the WHITE TRUCK from yesterday's dream—the truck that blocked my way until I learned what I was supposed to learn? Now a little piece of machinery is coming off of the big truck to do some heavy lifting. It's much more efficient than the big one. Funny how "smaller" can sometimes be more efficient for getting the job done . . .

*Aha!* How subtle—I could have easily missed this one. Is life really full of these minor synchronistic messages? Is my imagination creating this stuff, or have I been missing out on this world of affirmation and guidance? Not only does the outer life symbol of the "big truck and little machine" accurately reflect my dilemma over balancing my gifts, but it is also speaking about weighty synchronistic events (big truck) versus minor synchronistic occurrences (little machine)!

Back to the dreamwork. At the end of the dream about the MEAT symbol, I hear IN MY LEFT EAR SOMEONE TAKING A BITE OF AN APPLE. I think the literal meaning is that I need to add apples to my list of healthy foods to eat regularly. Since the sound I hear is on my left, I know that this information pertains to my inner awareness, my unconscious. If I look to the Bible, the bite of the apple caused Eve to become aware of Good and Evil. It opened the door for perceiving dualities—like positive and negative. It also led to getting thrown out of the garden to live this Human life with its joys and sorrows. Could the APPLE be a reminder of this metaphorical story of the Garden of Eden? Is it a symbol similar to the TREADMILL and its representation of my becoming separated from my inner self and God's guidance? Did my guilt over wayward behaviors cause me to hide from a God that I believed would be disappointed in me? Just as Adam and Eve did after they ate the forbidden fruit?

Symbolically, the BITE OF AN APPLE caused Snow White to fall asleep. Yet, now that I have noticed the truck outside, I wonder if this auditory symbol of the apple bite is saying, "Don't become unconscious of this new learning. Stay aware of *meaning* that is present around you." Wow, this gives me the kind of chills I get when I know something is true!

In working through this dream, another one of my life's patterns erupts: collecting or hoarding items I simply want or things I think will be used in the future. In the *FREE BEEF* dream the meat is collected, and it piles up. Just like my collecting and piling up things such as food, books, and projects in outer life. It's like the time I fell in love with knitting and couldn't pass the yarn aisle in a store without buying more yarn. When thinking of the five large garbage bags of yarn I eventually gave away, the pattern is so obvious. These actions reflect a fear that I won't get enough! Or it can translate into staying busy, keeping the TV and radio on, or finding plenty to do so I won't have to contend with the quiet, with the inner voice that might make me uncomfortable. In the *Pick 10* dream I am asked to "choose." Am I supposed to choose what is important enough to keep and therefore let go of everything else?

&#8766;&#8766;

Today I have noticed how I can carry my understanding of dream-symbols into outer life and apply it to the pictures and images that are hanging on my walls. It is clear to me why I am attracted to them. All have images that reflect a positive idea or quality or gift I am drawn to—a part of me. My Russell May print—the one of the small wooden cabin in the Smoky Mountains with snow on the ground and a full moon lighting up the evening scene—represents a place of refuge, of quiet solitude, of coziness and hominess. The smell of pines and the mountain air—I love this print. It brings to mind that early dream I had a few years ago, of the cozy apartment.

When searching the picture for any negative associations, I see the possibility of too much isolation, of not reaching out to be with friends, or staying insulated and not asking for help when needed. I see cold, lonely times and the rugged terrain of life. Oh, I can see the negative, but my vision quickly shifts back to the positive.

Is this a clue for me? Maybe I have learned to shut out the negative because of the obvious pain and discomfort. Perhaps I have adopted a "things will be all right" attitude, playing the "peacemaker" role to avoid conflict. I'm sure this is because I'm afraid of dealing with the scary, difficult stuff in life, such as growing up with an alcoholic father. My avoidance of conflict, the pain and discomfort of difficult things, and my feelings recede and hide in my unconscious . . . and go unresolved.

In taking time to observe a picture on my wall, I am amazed at what I have learned! I am beginning to see the significance of spending time with symbols, whether they are dream symbols or pictures and icons in waking life.

ॐ

As I progress through these dreams night after night, there seems to be a running commentary on my health, my eating habits, and my need for exercise. The first dream shows me a healthy cube of bread and the second suggests I eat apples and that I eat beef no more than twice a week. These subtle hints are imbedded in creative ways into dream scenarios that at first glance appear to have little to do with health.

Life is a process of *unlearning*. As the Holy Spirit works with me, I am learning to let go of what is unnecessary and to keep, and add to, what is vital and life-sustaining. The need to give myself time to be quiet, to surrender to Spirit, and to observe the inner and outer *meaning* that surrounds me is important.

It is becoming ever more clear to me that I might actually be learning through this dreamwork course how to reconnect with my deepest inner Self and re-establish a connection with God—just what I wished for on my "rainbow walk"! Does God give us dreams as a way of connecting to Divine guidance, knowing Earthly life is a confusing and difficult journey?

*Lessons I am Learning about Dreamwork*

**Lesson #8**

**Positive and Negative.** There is usually a positive and a negative aspect to symbols. I need to remember to look at both when doing the dreamwork.

**Lesson #9**

**Gifts.** Symbols that evoke a moderate or strong feeling might refer to my talents or spiritual gifts.

*. . . are [there] times when sleep becomes a sort of thin place where my soul meets the divine in a particular closeness, permitting a visionary sort of communication?*
**Molly Wolf**[1]

*Morning by morning he wakens—wakens my ear to listen as those who are taught.*
**Isaiah 50:4**[2]

*A world view that includes a belief in spiritual reality, however, would enable us to include the following.*
*1. God is always present, not only in the physical world but also in the spiritual world, which constantly breaks through into our consciousness via the dream and the vision.*
*2. God gives directions to those who are open to them.*
*3. We can directly confront and experience this spiritual world.*
*4. God is much more anxious to communicate with us than we are to listen.*
**Morton Kelsey**[3]

Chapter 8

# A Message from the Past

Dreams: *Pyramid Toaster; Marcy's Home*

## March 3, 2007

This strange new realm of *meaning* has me captivated. There seems to be an interweaving of the dreams and my daily life. Does Jung's concept of synchronicity and meaningful coincidences explain what I am experiencing? The dreams of the last two days make me wonder if dreams give clues about upcoming events. The WHITE TRUCK dream seems related to the "big truck, little machine" waking event that came yesterday. Hmm . . . I almost wrote "the big truck, little machine *real* event," but I'm not sure anymore what *is* the real world. Was the big truck outside my window the outer manifestation of the WHITE TRUCK from my dream? Could it be that the inner world, of which dreams may only be a part, is every bit as real as the outer physical world? My understanding is that there is no space/time in the inner realms, as there is in the outer, physical world. So . . . can dreams speak to past, current, or future events?

In the first dream this morning, several messages were given.

I AM TAKING A TAG, LIKE A SALES TAG ON AN ANTIQUE, OFF OF A SLICE OF BREAD TO TOAST

IT—TO EAT. I HAVE AN OVEN BUT NO TOASTER, SO I CLIMB ON A CHAIR TO GET A MELMAC PLATE ON WHICH TO PUT THE BREAD SO I CAN PLACE IT IN THE OVEN, BUT I KNOW ONLY ONE SIDE WILL TOAST. I LOOK FOR BUT CAN'T FIND A TOASTER LIKE GRANDMA HAD—THE PYRAMID KIND THAT TOASTS ON ONE SIDE. THERE ISN'T ONE UNDER THE CUPBOARDS.

The SALES TAG LIKE A SALES TAG ON AN ANTIQUE makes me think of Adrian and the antiques he sells. . . so maybe the dream has to do with him. Yesterday when he was pushed to remember his dreams and he remembered a small segment of one, I tried to "read" it to give him an interpretation. The SLICE OF BREAD might be referring to *his* small dream segment yesterday that I wanted to EAT—to digest, to interpret.

But in the dream I know that the OVEN—the way to cook the dream—will only cook it on one side, and so, perhaps, it is the wrong method. My guessing at what Adrian's dream means only gives my side of it, my limited interpretation, and not *his* truth. I know that MELMAC is plastic and certainly cannot be used in an oven or it will melt. MELMAC is cheap and it won't hold up, just as my interpretation of Adrian's dream cannot hold up.

At this point I should be able to see that my attempt to interpret Adrian's dream will end in disaster if I proceed. But I still don't get it! I'm only concerned that if I use the OVEN, it will only TOAST the BREAD on ONE SIDE. So, frustrated and wanting answers, I look for the PYRAMID TOASTER that belongs to Grandma. It, too, only toasts on one side, and then the bread has to be turned over to toast the other side. This appliance only does part of the job, too. But . . . the PYRAMID TOASTER can't be found.

This is another open-ended dream that has me questioning my actions. I think the dream is cautioning me against interpreting anyone else's dreams, including Adrian's. It makes sense that only the dreamer can know what his or her images and symbols mean . . .

Something happened last night that I thought of: When we went out to dinner for Kelly's birthday, my old co-worker, Connie, was sitting at the table next to us. I hadn't seen her in fifteen or twenty years. One of my strongest memories of her is about that time I tried to use remote viewing and healing to make suggestions about some medical symptoms she was having. My intentions were only for her good, but I still feel so uncomfortable about how wrong my interpretation was . . .

*Aha!* This memory gives *meaning* and emphasis to the idea that, as much as I might want to help another person, the person doing the dreaming is the only one who can accurately interpret what the dream might mean. If I try to do it, it will most likely be incorrect information.

Learning the important lesson of not interpreting anyone else's dream is crucial. It is challenging enough to interpret my own. The sequence of 1) trying to interpret Adrian's dream yesterday (my *mistake*), 2) seeing Connie at dinner later that night (a *synchronistic event*), 3) having the PYRAMID TOASTER *dream* this morning, and 4) later recalling the uncomfortable *memory* of long ago giving Connie the wrong interpretation (*Aha!*), all tie together to teach me this lesson. Whew.

Here is a second, tiny, dream segment from last night that I remember:

> A DREAM CHARACTER ASKS IF I WANT TO OPEN
> UP A GROCERY STORE. I SAY "No."

Does the grocery store represent a place of off-the-shelf interpretations—like those in a dream encyclopedia book? Does my saying "NO" foretell that I will figure out the message of the PYRAMID TOASTER dream?

❧

My head is spinning today, literally and figuratively. Literally, I have been having so many headaches, which I suspect are from these intense days of dreaming and dreamwork. It's as if my body can't keep up with the fast pace of what is happening to me, with all this understanding flooding in and all this work being put forth into the dreams. Figuratively, there are so many thoughts going through my brain that it's all I can do to remember them and write them down. It's not merely the two hours of dreamwork writing every morning—I am also seeing connections during the day, the interweaving of daytime events with the dreams from the night before, and trying to get those written down as well. I walk, eat, look, and talk in my outer world, but always there's a part of me that is immersed in the inner world at the same time. It's consuming, like being in a new relationship and in love. I have to trust that my new life with dreams and synchronicity will gradually settle down into a less intense energy flow.

Another dream from last night is making me uneasy. That Native American theme is emerging again, and I am concerned about being taken in a direction that will leave me stranded without my Christian framework. Christianity has grounded me in a way nothing else ever has; I don't want to be pulled away from it.

*In a house in town, I am visiting Marcy — a friend from church. She is a pleasant woman, simple, warm, down-to-earth. She has a rambling house with lots of family. I have to go to the bathroom. Marcy says, "Well . . . if it's, you know, a number $_2$, go upstairs." I go upstairs and try to find the bathroom. It looks like a white seat on the ground in a play area of a little park. Kids are all around. It is open — not an enclosed bathroom. I know I don't want to sit down with these kids here, but, more than that, I don't see how this is even a workable toilet. An older man, who looks Native American, says it is a recyclable one — where waste is composted and used as fertilizer. But it looks sealed up. There is no open hole for waste to drop down a pipe to wherever it should go. I notice that the entire upstairs has pools of water everywhere — several inches on the floor and all around the furniture. But it doesn't seem to hurt anything. I tell the kids that all of this water is heavy for their ceiling to hold. "You must have good sturdy construction!" I am amazed! I go downstairs to find a regular toilet. I had kept track of how*

*I FOUND THE UPSTAIRS SO I COULD FIND MY WAY DOWN AGAIN BY REMEMBERING THE WALLPAPER. I DON'T WANT TO SPY, BUT I CAN'T HELP NOTICING PLANTS ALL OVER THE HOUSE. I WONDER WHAT THEY ARE. I LIKE THIS LADY. SHE MUST REALLY HAVE A GREEN THUMB! SHE SEEMS TO BE A NURTURER. AGAIN, I NOTICE THAT THERE ARE AT LEAST THREE OR FOUR GENERATIONS OF FAMILY IN EVERY ROOM!*

This is the first hint in my dreamwork that I have somehow turned a corner—that new things are about to begin:

In the dream Marcy directs me UPSTAIRS (higher level of spiritual learning), but perhaps the SEAT ON THE GROUND also symbolizes the outer physical world. The seat is WHITE (holy) and set on the earth, not a man-made toilet. It is in a PARK (the park theme again!)—a social place where people play, live, and hike. The PARK theme makes me think of the park at the Fort Ancient archaeological site, which is so close to where we live. Not being A WORKABLE TOILET might mean that my work is mostly finished with expelling the old baggage that has blocked my spiritual growth. The OLDER MAN, who is NATIVE AMERICAN in appearance, says the toilet is a RECYCLABLE one, where waste (and old memories) are COMPOSTED AND USED AS FERTILIZER—turned into material for growth and used for good purposes. This is the first time a dream addresses any concept that goes further than merely expelling waste—letting go of old baggage. But I still don't quite get it. I expect to see a place to deposit waste to get rid of it, and this SEAT has no means to do that. Hmmmm . . .

I wonder if this has anything to do with the presentation that Marcy is giving at church later today?

$$\approx \infty$$

I've just returned from Marcy's presentation. She discussed her new book, *Singing the Moon into the Sky*.[4] In Marcy's talk, she mentioned that the burial place of the Shawnee Indian Leader, Tecumseh, has never been located. As I sat and listened to her, I felt the chills of an *Aha!* moment. I remembered the PYRAMID TOASTER from my dream this morning! Some Native Americans buried their leaders in pyramids. In the dream I couldn't find the PYRAMID TOASTER. Marcy told us that the burial place of Tecumseh cannot be found. I'm not sure if that itself is meaningful, but I do see the connection between the dream symbol and this outer life moment that came after it (not before it). But that was not all. Marcy went on to tell us about her work on her own genealogy, which includes her Native American heritage. No one, including myself, had any idea that she would be speaking on this or that she was doing genealogy.

Did my dream of seeing LOTS OF FAMILY, THREE OR FOUR GENERATIONS OF FAMILY, in the rooms of her house foretell the kind of information she would share today? As she spoke, she touched dried sage with a match, and a pleasant-smelling smoke filled the room. She said that sage smoke has a purifying effect and connects us to our higher power. It carries our thoughts to the Spirit Beings and ancestors. Do the plants that I saw in the dream of Marcy's house represent sage? Or the tobacco she mentioned that is offered as a gift to the Indian spirits?

The WHITE TRUCK, the PYRAMID TOASTER, and the GENERATIONS OF FAMILY dream images all refer to events in the *future*, not the past. The first symbol foretold of an actual future event—the big truck on the road—and the latter two foreshadowed subjects from Marcy's talk—Tecumseh's grave and her genealogy work.

Marcy's talk was enjoyable, but I am still uneasy about the rise of this new Native American theme. I don't want this dreamwork to pull me off my Christian track. But then, the talk *was* given in the *church*, after all. And Marcy *is* joining my Bible study group. So maybe the Holy Spirit wants us to join Native American spirituality together somehow with our Christian spirituality.

Hmmm . . . Now I am feeling curious about, and not quite as threatened by, the Native American threads that are weaving through some of my dreams and waking life: the Indian heads, the ancestors, the Indian man in *MARCY'S HOME*, and Marcy's increasing presence in my outer life. It seems that my interest in Native American themes earlier in my life is being woven back into my current spiritual life. This is starting to catch my interest. I can't wait to see where this takes me!

*Lessons I am Learning about Dreamwork*

**Lesson #10**

**Dream Symbols are Personal**. Only the dreamer knows for sure what his or her own dream symbols represent. To try to interpret someone else's dreams might result in misinterpretation.

**Lesson # 11**

**Prophetic Dreams**. Occasionally, one of the words, part of an image or the image itself appears in the future in outer life. Seeing the symbol in a dream, then seeing it in outer life, says "Pay attention!" to that special moment. It may give insight or lead to action.

*In the first place, we must overcome the tendency to think of ourselves as exclusively masculine or feminine . . .*
**John A. Sanford**[1]


*So we do not lose heart.*
*Even though our outer nature is wasting away,*
*our inner nature is being renewed day by day.*
**2 Corinthians 4:16**[2]


*The strength of the John* tradition is that it produces a spirituality that sees God in the whole of life and regards all things as inter-related.*
**J. Philip Newell**[3]
*The Gospel of John

Chapter 9

# Letting Go of Guilt

Dreams: *On Eagle's Wings Melody; Atop the J.C. Penney Store/Train Wreck; The Director's Chair*

## March 4, 2007

Dream symbols can come in different forms. They can come as spoken words in my head, like the voice that said, "You okay, Tink?" And, of course they can come as objects like a TREADMILL, or the WHITE SEAT ON THE GROUND in yesterday's dream. In this morning's dream, a symbol came in the form of a melody. I woke up hearing the hymn "On Eagle's Wings." The lyrics come from Psalm 91, and I find them pertinent and comforting:

> "AND I WILL RAISE YOU UP ON EAGLE'S WINGS,
> BEAR YOU ON THE BREATH OF DAWN, MAKE
> YOU TO SHINE LIKE THE SUN, AND HOLD YOU
> IN THE PALM OF MY HAND."[4]

Is this hymn and its familiar words about trust suggesting to me that I will need to have a greater measure of trust as I go forward? Is my short course in dreamwork going to get more challenging?

After hearing the hymn, I fell back to sleep and had a very long dream, with a smaller segment at the end:

*I AM DRIVING TO DAYTON MALL. IT IS LATE AND DARK. I AM ALONE AND CAN HARDLY SEE. I HAVE TO BUY A PAIR OF BLACK SLACKS. I FIND THE SIDE ENTRANCE TO THE J.C. PENNEY STORE. I WALK IN THE STAIRS AREA AND ASK A PERSON HOW TO GET TO THE MAIN FLOOR. SHE TAKES ME UPSTAIRS. IT DOESN'T SEEM TO BE THE RIGHT PLACE, SO I GO ON UP THE STAIRS AND COME OUT ONTO THE ROOF OF THE BUILDING, WHICH SEEMS TO BE A GRASSY COURTYARD. IT IS DAYLIGHT. THERE ARE MILITARY MEN, AS THOUGH THIS IS AN ARMY RESERVE AREA. I WALK CONFIDENTLY ACROSS THE GRASSY ROOF TO WHERE SOME OUTBUILDINGS ARE. I WALK IN FRONT OF A SOLDIER IN UNIFORM WITH A RIFLE POINTED IN MY DIRECTION. I'M NOT AFRAID, BUT SURPRISED. I WALK INTO ONE OF THE BUILDINGS AND ASK A SOLDIER HOW I CAN GET TO A DIFFERENT FLOOR BACK IN THE WHITE J.C. PENNEY STORE. THE MAN SAYS THAT I SHOULD GO TO THE MAIN LOBBY WHERE THE MARQUEE OR DIRECTORY FOR THE STORE IS LOCATED. I KNEW HE WOULD TELL ME HOW TO GET THERE. WHEN I WALK BACK ACROSS THE YARD, I REALIZE THAT J.C. PENNEY, THE WHITE BUILDING, IS UNDERNEATH ME. I'M NOT LOST. I AM CLOSE AND JUST NEED TO FIND THE ELEVATOR OR STAIRWAY DOWN TO IT.*

In the dream I am driving to *DAYTON MALL AT NIGHT* in search of *BLACK PANTS* from the *J.C. PENNEY STORE*. It seems as if I am in the dark about the next phase of dreamwork. Or perhaps I am to learn about a shadow part of me. Literally, *BLACK PANTS* seems to refer to a pair of black slacks that I need to wear for singing in the choir during the Lenten season. Symbolically, BLACK can be the color of the feminine, but PANTS is a masculine image. Perhaps this dream is pointing to a time when I either had to use or will have to use more masculine attributes—logic, organization, decision-making—to get things done.

The *J.C.* seems to refer to Jesus Christ; the *J. C. PENNEY STORE* is a place with a wide variety of selections. Is the dream trying to say to me that Christianity can contain a variety of spiritual practices? Maybe.

In the next segment I enter the store by a SIDE ENTRANCE that puts me in an employee stairwell with a young woman. It seems as if this particular Christianity is behind the scenes—not the mainstream, well-used path. Someone shows me how to go UPSTAIRS (higher spiritual learning), and eventually I come out ON THE ROOF, outside, on top of the *J.C. PENNEY* building. It is now DAYLIGHT. I have moved from a place of darkness into a place of light. As my dreamwork continues, I take this to mean I am in a higher spiritual realm for purposes of instruction. The surroundings look more like a grassy outdoor place than a roof. I recognize that this is an *ARMY RESERVE AREA*. The SOLDIERS are masculine helpers, but there aren't a whole lot of them around. Walking CONFIDENTLY, tells me that I am comfortable in this masculine area. A soldier who is pointing a gun in my direction does not instill any fear. Why am I so at ease up here in this masculine world? I proceed to a SMALL OUTBUILDING and ask a SOLDIER how to get to a DIFFERENT FLOOR back in the *J.C. PENNEY* building. I am still concerned with 1) looking for the BLACK SLACKS—though not yet knowing the symbolic meaning; and 2) wanting to stay within the realm of Christianity. He tells me I can go to the LOBBY and I will find a MARQUEE or a DIRECTORY. The interpretation may be that this DIRECTORY will show me "the Way"—how to get to where I want to go—to my traditional Christian roots. I also suspect that this sign might be an announcement of other spiritual options. But the word "marquee" is interesting. I think of a marquee as being a large sign above a movie theater. Am I being prepared for some kind of show? Some sort of drama? As I WALKED ACROSS THE YARD on the roof, I realize that J.C. PENNEY— THE WHITE (holy) building is UNDERNEATH ME. The dream seems to reassure me that I won't get LOST. In yesterday's dream of the UPSTAIRS (higher spiritual level) of Marcy's house, I knew how to get back down by remembering the WALLPAPER, by remembering how I came UPSTAIRS. Now I realize that I know how to get where I want to go, by finding the ELEVATOR or STAIRWAY and checking the DIRECTORY.

It seems after three years of intense learning, reading, and praying, Christianity has become a foundation UNDERNEATH ME. I won't get LOST and don't have to be afraid of losing my way in this new endeavor. From this dream I realize that I can explore spiritual learning from a different perspective such as dreamwork and still trust that my Christian faith will support me!

In the next part of the dream:

> AS I STAND ON THE ROOF OF THE J.C. PENNEY STORE, I SEE A YOUNG WOMAN SITTING ON THE GRASS IN THE COURTYARD. SHE SEEMS TO KNOW ME, BUT AT FIRST I DON'T KNOW HER. WE TALK FOR A FEW MOMENTS. AS I TURN TO LEAVE, I SAY, "I'LL TELL THE OTHER SUPERVISOR THAT I SAW YOU." I SAY THIS TO

LET HER KNOW THAT I NOW REALIZE I KNOW HER FROM A CASE I HAD WORKED IN MY OLD CHILDREN'S PROTECTIVE SERVICES DAYS. I CAN SEE THAT SHE HAS GROWN UP AND IS DOING FINE. SHE SEEMS PLEASED THAT I FINALLY RECOGNIZE HER.

Even all these years later I still worry how the decisions I had to make at the children's protective service agency affected the children and their parents. The YOUNG WOMAN ON THE ROOF is Mindy, who was a pre-teen when she was placed in foster care. My behavior and response still bothers me from that day she came back to the agency as a young adult and asked to see me. I could have found out then how she had fared, but it was a missed opportunity because I told the secretary I was too busy. Truthfully, I was just plain scared.

Why was I afraid? I was used to dealing with all sorts of difficult situations and angry people—clients, attorneys, prosecutors, sexual offenders—yet I was afraid to find out how my work had affected this young one. Maybe she had only come to thank me, or maybe just to obtain some needed information out of her old file, not to yell at me as I had feared. I will likely never know. Reflecting back, I acted like such a coward, thinking of myself instead of her and what she might have needed.

This dream brings relief because in this dream, at least, she is doing fine. I find comfort in the hopeful thought that the young people whose lives were affected may be doing okay. I know I have been given this dream segment to help me let go of those agency days and my worries over the children and their parents.

There is yet more to this dream:

> I AM STILL ON THE J.C. PENNEY ROOF. I AM
> WATCHING A TRAIN WRECK IN SLOW MOTION,
> WITH THE TRAIN'S ENGINE AND CARS SLOWLY
> FALLING OVER WITH A NOISE LIKE THUNDER.
> I SEE A MAN WORKING WITH THE ENGINE
> AS IT FALLS OVER—OFF THE TRACK, IN MY
> DIRECTION, WITH A LOUD, LOUD NOISE THAT
> IS THUNDEROUS. I WATCH THIS SCENE REPLAY
> TWO MORE TIMES. I NOTICE THAT BY THE
> SECOND AND THIRD TIME, THE FALLING TRAIN
> IS BEING CONTROLLED BY DREAM HELPERS.
> THE SECOND TIME THE SOUND IS A BIT OFF
> FROM THE ACTION, AND I REALIZE SOMEONE IS
> ADDING THE SOUND FOR EFFECT. THE THIRD
> TIME, THERE IS NO SOUND—JUST THE TRAIN
> QUIETLY FALLING OVER.

Is it telling me that I might experience something that at first will feel like a setback, like being knocked OFF THE TRACK, but that I am to realize that it is staged, choreographed to help me with my journey? Am I still afraid that my Christian faith is off the track?

No, seeing that the TRAIN WRECK is choreographed, and that it is being guided, eases my mind, similar to the absolution felt from seeing that Mindy is doing well. Also, I am greatly comforted by the overall message of the J.C. PENNEY dream: that my Christian faith has a solid foundation.

After this dream, I have a second, separate, dream. It seems to be picking up the theme of my work at the protective service agency.

*I AM SITTING ON A DIRECTOR'S CHAIR IN A COURTROOM-LIKE AREA. THERE ARE SEVERAL DIRECTORS' CHAIRS. THEY ARE COLORFUL BUT VERY UNCOMFORTABLE. I WATCH AS A YOUNG MAN GIVES TESTIMONY. I AM IN THE PRESENCE OF THE JUDGE. THERE ARE FOUR OF US. I AM AWARE OF A YOUNG MAN BEHIND ME IN ONE OF THE CHAIRS. I TELL HIM OF MY DISCOMFORT IN THE CHAIR, AND I FINALLY GET OUT OF THE CHAIR AND PLOP DOWN ON THE FLOOR.*

This brings me back to the many times spent in a courtroom testifying and observing. Being a supervisor in charge of screening and investigations was like sitting in the *DIRECTOR'S CHAIR*. How increasingly *UNCOMFORTABLE* I became as the years went by.

When my *DISCOMFORT* is shared with my masculine counterpart, he is *BEHIND ME,* which could signify that this is a role I played in the past. He (my masculine side) does not seem to be bothered in the same way I am. *He* could handle twenty-two years of listening to the stories of children who were beaten and molested. *He* could handle making those hard decisions that left children in difficult situations and those that required children to be removed from the parents they loved. My softer, feeling, feminine side could not. I realize now that having to *JUDGE*—to make judgments in order to make decisions—took a great toll, not on my masculine side, but on my feminine side.

In the courtroom scene, my dreamself decides to get *OUT OF THE CHAIR, TO PLOP,* to relax, to rest on the *FLOOR*. The *FLOOR* is the base level, a place to restart—as if a child—to re-connect, to go back to basics; signifying that my days of being in the DIRECTOR'S CHAIR, in control, are over.

This dream is encouraging me to become a student again! Is there a new theme emerging? Am I being asked to get in touch with my feeling, feminine side—the one that has been repressed all these years?

၆ဝၚ

This afternoon I read how St. John used the number seven in Revelation many times. The number seven is considered to be holy; the Trinity plus the four directions or corners of the earth; "four different phases of the moon, each of which measures seven days; seven is a number of completion and fullness,"[5] . . . a totality: seven tribes, seven seals, and seven heavens.[6]

When I looked up this information in *Herders Dictionary of Symbols*, I was surprised to find that the receipt was still inside the book and the date on the receipt was from fourteen years ago. As I started to wonder if a fourteen-year passage of time is significant, I looked down and on that very page is a discussion of the number fourteen. "A number significant in Christian symbolism as the double of the sacred number seven, it is also the number of goodness and mercy."[7] The message is affirming that this is the perfect time for me to return to dreamwork, and that goodness and mercy are indeed with me.

There is so much wisdom in these dreams night after night. I am being taught to trust even more that the Holy Spirit is the designer of all dreamwork, that I am in the palm of His hand, just as the hymn I heard last night said. I won't get lost. I am being guided and prepared for the next phase of my journey . . .

*Lessons I am Learning about Dreamwork*

**Lesson #12**

**Forms.** Symbols come in different forms. They can appear as physical objects or they can come as something auditory such as music or spoken words.

**Lesson #13**

**Consolation.** Symbols answer deep concerns, feelings, and questions that I have from the prior day or even from the past.

*Without words we cannot tell stories.*
*We can hug and kiss, but we cannot say "I love you"*
*We can look at the glory of the sunrise or the brilliance*
*of the stars, but without words we cannot ask,*
*"Who made you?"*
*We cannot say, "Maker of the universe and of me,*
*I trust you." We can feel hunger or lust or fatigue,*
*but we cannot ask questions.*
**Madeleine L'Engle**[1]

*What a beautiful home, God of the Angel Armies!*
*I've always longed to live in a place like this,*
*Always dreamed of a room in your house,*
*where I could sing for joy to God-alive!*
**Psalm 84:1-2**[2]

*By the tender mercy of our God,*
*the dawn from on high will break upon us,*
*to give light to those who sit in darkness*
*and in the shadow of death,*
*to guide our feet into the way of peace.*
**Luke 1:78-79**[3]

Chapter 10

# The Religion Squeeze

Dream: *Table of Contents and the Too Small Upstairs*

## March 5, 2007

This morning's dream is the first dream where I am in a sort of instructional dialogue with a dream helper. He gives me direction, then I ask a question to clarify the information, and he responds.

> I AM STANDING ON THE FRONT PORCH OF A LITTLE HOUSE. I AM LISTING THE COST OF ITEMS, ITEMIZING THEM FOR A HELPER. I HAVE TWO SETS OF NUMBERS. I REALIZE THAT I FORGOT TO ADD IN AN ITEM WORTH 25 ON TOP AND ONE WORTH 50 ON THE BOTTOM. I WANT TO GET THE COLUMNS RIGHT, SO I CLEAN UP THE COLUMNS AND PUT THOSE NUMBERS IN SO THE HELPER CAN SEE THAT THEY ADD UP TO THE RIGHT NUMBER. I ASK THE HELPER IF I SHOULD LIST WHAT THE NUMBERS REPRESENT. HE SAYS, "YES, IT WOULD BE A GOOD IDEA SO THE ONE VIEWING THE LIST CAN SEE WHAT THE LIST IS IN REFERENCE TO: LIKE, LAMP . . . 25, HOUSE . . . 50, ETC." I NOW HAVE TWO SETS OF TEN NUMBERS.

What does LISTING THE COST mean? What do the numbers REPRESENT? Why are the items given different values or numbers? What is the helper trying to tell me about the paperwork? I certainly need help because it has gotten so overwhelming that there seem to be piles of it everywhere.

HOUSE is a symbol from recent dreams! The helper is instructing me to put the dreams in SETS OF TEN with the symbols they contain as a subset under each dream title. The dreams and their symbols should be given page numbers . . . it is a way to catalogue symbols so I can refer back to them. ADDING UP the column is not just a way to list (make a table of contents) and find a symbol and the dream it was in when I need it, but to also give a brief description of what the symbol means. That way, when the symbol appears in future dreams I can thumb through the ever-growing table of contents for a quick way to find the symbol and its meaning in past dreams.

To facilitate this I decide to punch holes in the dreamwork sheets and place them in a binder. When there are ten more new dreams, I will follow the same process. In addition, I'll put all the pages of material from meditations about dream content, and scriptural passages from Sunday services and Bible studies in the binder with the dream to which they refer.

The Holy Spirit must have realized how overwhelmed I became by all the information and paperwork the dreams have been producing! I am so thankful for the dream helper's information. From past experience I know that because dreams are from the realm of the unconscious, they soon fade back into the unconscious. Now I have a method to keep track of them.

৶৶৹

In the same dream, the helper tells me to leave my paperwork on the GRAY WOODEN PORCH FLOOR and go in the HOUSE.

> NOW I AM IN THE HOUSE . . . TINY, CUTE, AND FRESHLY WALLPAPERED—AT LEAST THE UPSTAIRS IS. I CLIMB UP THE STAIRS AND THE UPSTAIRS SEEMS SO SMALL—TIGHT QUARTERS, I CAN HARDLY MOVE AROUND. I WONDER, "HOW DID GRANDMA AND GRANDPA EVER LIVE HERE?" I REMEMBER THAT I NEED TO LOCK THE DOORS DOWNSTAIRS IF I HADN'T ALREADY DONE SO. IT SEEMS THE MORE I TRY TO MOVE AROUND, THE SMALLER THE UPSTAIRS BECOMES. IT HAS COLORFUL FLOWERED WALLPAPER, BUT I CAN JUST BARELY SQUEEZE THROUGH THE OPENING TO GET DOWNSTAIRS. I MAKE IT . . . AND CHECK THE DOORS. THEY ARE LOCKED. I AM RELIEVED TO BE DOWN OUT OF THE ATTIC—THE SECOND FLOOR—BECAUSE OF ITS TIGHT QUARTERS. IT IS NIGHT—DARK OUTSIDE. I KNOW THE DREAM HELPER IS COMING TO SEE IF I HAVE LOCKED THE DOORS.

The second message of this dream seems to continue the theme of incorporating expanded spiritual ideas into my Christian thinking. The PORCH is a few feet up from ground level, perhaps to represent progress in my journey. The house appears to belong to GRANDMA AND GRANDPA. THE WOODEN PORCH is painted GRAY, just as I remember theirs was . . .

Since GRANDMA AND GRANDPA are part of my previous married life, this little house seems to represent a belief system that is no longer workable. The DOWNSTAIRS is roomy enough, but the UPSTAIRS (my higher spiritual level), although COLORFUL and FLOWERY, and a place someone cared about and for, is growing too TIGHT for me.

This is the third time in three days that I have seen an UPSTAIRS image in my dreams! The first was the UPSTAIRS in MARCY'S HOME, a place of grass and nature, a park-like setting with pools of water, children, and a dream-helper. The second was the ROOF of the J.C. PENNEY building, which was an outdoor setting with grass in the daytime. It had people and several dream-helpers. This morning, the UPSTAIRS is in marked contrast to the first two. Although it has COLORFUL FLOWERED WALLPAPER, it is too confining. Its flowers are wallpaper flowers. It is definitely not an outdoor setting. It has no dream-helpers and is clearly not a comfortable place anymore.

In the dream I feel like a man seen on TV last night. He claimed to be crawling in and out of what he believed was Jesus' family tomb. It was a cramped space. Is this what this shrinking attic bedroom is about? Do I have too narrow a view of Christ? Is Christ much more than what I can ever imagine?

In the dream I can HARDLY MOVE AROUND. Is my knowledge of and faith in Christianity so confining that I can't grow or experience new thinking? Will looking at new ideas like Native American symbolism and spirituality cause me to exclude or abandon the Christianity I have rediscovered? Or, is it possible to incorporate the new with the traditional?

This balancing, this stepping out from the known, is making me anxious. In my youth I remember how becoming sexually active closed off my Catholic faith and created internal tension. I couldn't reconcile my sexual behavior with my religion and with being a good girl. Aha! Does exploring non-traditional spiritual beliefs and practices mean being a bad girl and represent a cutting off of my faith?

When the Mass was changed from Latin to English, I remember how GRANDMA AND GRANDPA cut off their faith and stopped going. They couldn't grow with the Church. They stayed in their small-house way of thinking. I am curious about the dream helper coming to see if I have LOCKED THE DOORS. It appears that the Holy Spirit intends for me to move on not only from my past memories, but also from my current spiritual beliefs.

> I AM IN A CAR PARKED IN A CIRCLE OR CUL-DE-SAC OUT IN THE FRONT OF THE HOUSE. THERE ARE OTHER CARS PARKED THERE ALSO. I LET ALL THE OTHER CARS GO OUT OF THEIR PARKING PLACES IN A LINE OUT TO THE ROAD, AND I PULL OUT IN BACK OF THEM ALL, BRINGING UP THE REAR. ALL THE CARS ARE NOW OUT OF THE CIRCULAR DRIVE.

After I LOCK THE DOORS to the little house, I find myself in front of it in a CAR PARKED IN A CUL-DE-SAC with other waiting cars. It appears I am closing the door on my small-house way of thinking and starting a journey with a group of people who are also expanding their own spiritual thinking, which is true of my Saturday Bible-study group. In a broader sense, I am now traveling the path of all seekers who study and follow the wisdom in their dreams. Following the cars out of the CUL-DE-SAC, a confining dead-end place, to a main ROAD on the journey, represents ending an era of narrow thinking. The dream is telling me it is time to move on . . . to explore and to grow. But move on to where?

⋙⋘

After organizing all the paperwork as instructed in the dream, I've discovered two things:

1. The number I assigned to represent the WORTH of each ITEM (symbols) in the dream is not just a page number as I had first thought. The WORTH of each symbol is based on its power to instruct, help, and heal.

2. With the paperwork organized and the table of contents established, it appears that the dreams seem to be coming in chapters . . .

⋙⋘

The dreams I've had of forgiveness, and those that brought to light my fears about becoming apathetic toward my Christian faith, have built the foundation for these new dreams of insight and learning. The Holy Spirit seems to be preparing me to see the Divine in a more expansive way. God is helping me get over the fear of getting lost, both behaviorally and spiritually, by giving me an understanding of what happened in the past.

This theme, about my concern of deviating from what I believe to be Christian faithfulness, has been addressed in different ways over several dreams. Now, it seems it is time to move on.

Through my dreams and dreamwork, the Holy Spirit is dispelling my fears and instilling trust, changing my anxiety to excitement! What is actually happening is the opposite of what I feared: Scripture readings and Bible verses are *more* meaningful as a result of this work. Christ's words are *more* relevant to me. It's as if the Divine is continually saying: "DO NOT BE AFRAID. God is in control of this journey."

*Lessons I am Learning about Dreamwork*

**Lesson #14**

**Themes**. Dreams often come in chapters. A theme may occur over several nights of dreaming, or several weeks, or longer. The overall focus is to heal and instruct.

**Lesson #15**

**Guidance**. Symbols can indicate when it is time to move on, and they help ease my fears and anxiety over new changes.

*The experience of God is the experience of the
Mystery that governs our lives
from within and without.*
**Raimon Panikker**[1]

*Return to the Lord your God,
for He is gracious and merciful,
slow to anger, and abounding in steadfast love.*
**Joel 2:13**[2]

*The real danger of not treating the creative imagination
with real love is that this
involves a rejection of God—or at least of a huge and
magnificent dimension of God.*
**Sara Maitland**[3]

Chapter 11

# Don't Block the Process!

Dreams: *The Big Man in the White T-Shirt; The Too Small Upstairs . . .*
*continued*

## March 7, 2007

Today is Wednesday. Yesterday I couldn't remember my dreams. It was because I got up early to go over to Kelly's to watch Ella and William. Being with the children gave me a break from this dreamwork that has me so absorbed. After Monday's dream of locking the HOUSE with the TOO SMALL UPSTAIRS, I am curious to see where Spirit will take me next.

The first dream segment this morning:

> THERE ARE TWO BUILDINGS ON EITHER SIDE
> OF A RAVINE. I WALK THROUGH THE BUILDING
> ON THE LEFT, DOWN A HALL. A BIG MAN IN A
> WHITE T-SHIRT WALKS UP TO ME, WANTING TO
> BE MY FRIEND. I SAY HE CAN BE MY FRIEND AS
> LONG AS IT IS PLATONIC. HE AGREES. I SAY, "I
> DON'T EVEN WANT TO HEAR YOU SAY, 'GIVE ME
> A KISS ON THE CHEEK'!" HE AGREES. LATER, AS
> I COME OUT OF AN AUDITORIUM DOOR, I SEE
> HIM AND HE GRINS AND SAYS "GIVE ME A KISS
> RIGHT HERE," AS HE POINTS TO HIS CHEEK. I
> AM FURIOUS AND I EXPLODE. I SAY THAT HE

CANNOT "HANG OUT" WITH ME. THAT IT IS
NOT THE IDEA OF A KISS . . . IT IS THE BROKEN
TRUST. HE HAS NOT KEPT HIS WORD. I REFUSE
TO LET HIM BE WITH ME, THOUGH HE TRIES TO
TALK ME INTO BEING FRIENDS. I AM ADAMANT
ABOUT NOT BEING ABLE TO TRUST HIM.

The image of the TWO BUILDINGS ON EITHER SIDE OF A
RAVINE seems to set up an issue. Maybe TWO BUILDINGS
implies two ways of thinking? Or simply, the buildings
could represent the inner and outer worlds since they
seem to be on my left and right. Maybe . . . but they are
also divided by a ravine—which suggests that they are not
compatible. I feel as if I'm guessing here. I need to continue
writing questions about the dream . . .

When I first woke up from this dream, I felt angry
with the T-SHIRT MAN symbol. Why? Does it indicate
that I am fighting against something that I still need to
figure out and understand? The dream is showing me
that my anger or resistance may be blocking something
important. But what?

On the conscious level, I think this segment has to do
with Allen because after reminding him of something he
promised to keep to himself, he didn't. But I know that
isn't the whole explanation. Who is the BIG MAN in the
WHITE (holy) T-SHIRT? What does he represent?

The dream continued:

I LEAVE BY A ROAD I SEE IN THE DISTANCE TO
GO TO THE SCHOOL BUILDING ON THE RIGHT
SIDE OF THE RAVINE. IT IS A NEW BUILDING,

BUILT RECENTLY. IT SEEMS THAT IT IS IN THE
AMERICAN SOUTHWEST AND CANNOT HAVE
A BASEMENT BECAUSE OF THE HARD, ROCKY
GROUND. I GO IN THE BUILDING AND SIT AT A
TABLE WITH TWO PEOPLE. DAVID WALKS IN. WE
HAVEN'T BEEN A COUPLE IN A LONG TIME BUT I
HOPE HE WILL SIT WITH US OR ACKNOWLEDGE
US. HE WALKS ON BY.

In this dream segment, I am so angry with the T-SHIRT
MAN that I leave this LEFT (inner) SIDE and go to the BUILDING
on the other side of the RAVINE. It is NEW, RECENTLY BUILT,
on ROCKY GROUND in the SOUTHWEST. Hmmm . . . maybe
the image of a NEW BUILDING on my RIGHT (outer), on
Southwestern ground, refers to the Carlos Castanada
dream book I have been skimming.[4] But, the building can't
have a BASEMENT BECAUSE OF THE HARD, ROCKY GROUND—
it is bumpy, inflexible, difficult, and not safe or reliable.
*Aha!* Carlos Castanada lacks the *foundation* I want; there
is no mention of the Divine in his work and I don't sense
any spiritual underpinning in the book. His way of doing
dreamwork is a method I do not want to learn.

Perhaps I should hesitate before being too critical since
I have not read all of his books. However, it feels to me as
if his goal is dreamwork itself, to become like his mentor,
Don Juan, rather than to use his dreamwork to listen to God
or to develop a closer relationship with the Holy Spirit.

The next dream segment really brings this home:

I AM IN A CAR DRIVING AT NIGHT. I STOP IN
A CARPORT IN FRONT OF MY OLD BOYFRIEND
DAVID'S HOUSE, AND THROUGH THE HOUSE

> WINDOW I SEE HIS CAR PULLING UP OUT BACK.
> I TURN MY IGNITION OFF AND TAKE OUT MY
> KEYS. WHEN I LOOK DOWN ON THE SEAT,
> THERE IS ANOTHER SET OF KEYS, BUT I DON'T
> KNOW WHAT THEY ARE FOR, SO I LEAVE THEM
> IN THE CAR. I GET OUT OF THIS CAR AND INTO
> ANOTHER CAR PARKED NEXT TO IT.

The DAVID memory takes me back to when I was living without any Divine connection and my life was full of destructive ways of thinking. In the dream, I am watching him and I see TWO SETS OF KEYS in the CAR. I recognize I have a choice. To stay and continue my dead-end way of thinking, or choose to TURN OFF THE IGNITION and get into the other CAR, so that I can advance on my spiritual journey. . . an easy choice. Thank goodness!

DAVID is left behind and I continue on:

> I AM DRIVING DOWN COLUMBIA PARKWAY
> HEADING EAST. I SEE A PRISM IN THE CLOUDS
> OVER THE RIVER TO MY RIGHT. KELLY IS IN
> THE BACKSEAT. KELLY SHOUTS, "THERE'S THE
> HAWK!" I LOOK UP AND SEE A BIG BIRD LAND
> ON THE ROCKY HILLSIDE TO MY LEFT. KELLY
> SAYS SHE HAS SEEN THIS HAWK BEFORE AT THIS
> VERY SPOT. I NOTICE THAT THE COLOR OF ITS
> BACK IS TOO DARK FOR A HAWK.

On my Crossroads/Quadrants Map, EAST takes me deeper into the unconscious spiritual realm. The PRISM lets me know I am back on my "rainbow" journey. Since the HAWK has been seen before AT THIS VERY SPOT, I think it is a symbol of the past. It hasn't progressed — it has returned to the same SPOT, that same hard, ROCKY GROUND as the BUILDING on the RIGHT SIDE OF THE RAVINE. Following this symbol will not help me progress. I am suspicious of this bird for another reason: the beautiful hawk often seen in our neighborhood is red-tailed and creamy-beige, not black. The BIRD is misrepresenting itself, trying to pass itself off as something it is not. I am now more sure than ever that Carlos Castanada's writing is not the right vehicle for the Native American symbolism that has been occurring in my life, visions, and dreams.

❧◦❧

After doing the dreamwork this morning I still wanted to know more about the BIG MAN IN THE WHITE T-SHIRT. So, just as I have done with themes and characters when writing for the church's newsletter or for writing class, I decided to just let him "live in my head" for a bit. I said a prayer to the Holy Spirit for help and guidance, quieted my mind, relaxed, and meditated. When I saw the T-SHIRT MAN clearly in my mind's eye, I asked the big guy "Who are you?" He replied that he represents Native American symbolism and spirituality! I was surprised, but it makes sense. I see that the WHITE T-SHIRT represents holy, yet informal spirituality as opposed to traditional, mainstream-religion spirituality.

He also told me that I have been attempting to call the shots, to control his behavior, to decide how I want *him* to interact with *me*. I feel as if the message from this powerful symbol says, "You, Candy, are not in control. If you don't let the process unfold as God intends, even if that takes you to unfamiliar places, you will be on the other side of the RAVINE, resorting to old ways of thinking, and you'll undo what progress you have made." Whoa! I gratefully and humbly thanked the Holy Spirit for this message.

As I reflected on the message, I re-read what I had written in my dream journal after recording the dream this morning: "As I got up and came back from the bathroom, I heard the melody and words of a piece of liturgical music in my head: *Return to the Lord your God, for He is merciful, slow to anger, and abounding in steadfast love.*"[5]

Again I am reminded that I am *not* in charge . . . God is. It's a good thing.

Ha! Just as I wrote that last passage, the soulful Celtic song playing on the CD player stuttered. It was stuck. What a synchronistic reminder that *I* will be stuck if I don't listen and stay open!

Whew. How much clearer a message can a stubborn, controlling woman be given?

*Lessons I am Learning about Dreamwork*

**Lesson #16**

**Strong Reactions.** Reacting strongly to a dream character or symbol by walking away, running, fighting, or ignoring it are clues to pay attention— that something significant is emerging. If I meditate on the symbol that caused the strong reaction and ask it what it represents, it may reveal a whole area that needs to be examined and healed.

**Lesson #17**

**Music.** Insight or meaning may come from music I hear in my mind during waking time. If I pay attention, I can see that the words relate to and interweave with an ongoing dream theme and speak to the issue at hand.

# PART IV

# HEALING

There is a potentially unbroken continuity of experience stretching from the ordinary, limited awareness of "me" (my seemingly small and separate waking "self"), all the way to a transcendent awareness of completeness and oneness and self-identification with the ALL—the Divine. In my experience, all dreams are ultimately aimed at this transcendent, direct, conscious, creative participation in the collective archetypal, divine energies that are given shape in the cosmic dance of all life. At the very least, this is a way of conceptualizing the scope of the complete, transpersonal "health and wholeness" toward which our dreams are always striving.

**Jeremy Taylor**[1]

So if anyone is in Christ, there is a new creation:
everything old has passed away;
see, everything has become new!
**2 Corinthians 5:17**[2]

There are patterns of transformation in which we find ourselves confronted by the very issues we sought to avoid or escape during earlier stages of development. This cyclical process of encounter and reencounter is a deep feature of emergent being—every stage is played out, if necessary, over and over, until the necessary lessons or insights are learned and fully integrated. We must revisit the territory and proving grounds of our younger self, visit all the places or vulnerabilities in order to move beyond them through transformation into a more integral and complete life.

**Lee Irwin**[3]

Chapter 12

# Rescuing the Feminine

Dreams: *The Veil of Moonlight; The Green and White Garbage Truck*

**March 8, 2007**

To help deal with my qualms about the emerging Native American theme, I wrote down a question last night before bed, hoping the answer would come in my dreams: "Will symbols/myths from spiritual traditions other than Christianity enhance my relationship with God?"

Upon waking at 12:38 a.m. I heard these words in my head: "HOW DO THEY HOLD UP WHEN SEEN THROUGH THE VEIL OF MOONLIGHT?" What? I knew the dream voice was trying to tell me how to look at symbols, but I didn't fully understand the question. When I fell back to sleep, I again woke with the voice telling me to look at symbols THROUGH PRISM COLORS. Oh! I get it—colors!

It's an obscure idea, but I do understand it. Through writing the articles on each month's liturgy for the church newsletter, I have developed an increased understanding of the language of colors . . . each liturgical season has an associated color that represents the focus of the season: Advent's color is blue and represents hope, Christmas is white for holiness, Easter's color is gold to represent the majesty of the most important liturgical celebration of the year, and Pentecost is green, the color of growth and abundance.

If those colors represent ideas and concepts, then what the dream voice might be saying is that the colors in my dreams may also have meanings, and if I understand those meanings, it will help me with my dream interpretations.

Further, if the color concepts such as hope, holiness, and growth are universal and common to the outer world as seen in the church, and the inner world as evidenced in dreams, then the dream voice seems to be implying that I can assess images from other spiritual traditions by looking at them through the dream color concepts:[4]

**Red** - passion, vitality, strength

**Orange** - understanding, warmth, joy, creativity, caution

**Yellow** - communication, optimism

**Green** - growth, healing, abundance, newness, not yet ripe

**Blue** - truth, hope, calmness

**Indigo** - clear vision, helping one to "see"

**Violet** - spirit, loyalty, royalty

**White** – pure, holy

Wow! Now there is yet another way of interpreting inner dream symbols as well as other non-Christian spiritual ideas—I can use the prism definitions. If I apply my new understanding of the qualities associated with colors—truthfulness, hopefulness, creativity, etc.—to inner and outer symbols, will the interpretations help me have a clearer, more colorful vision to guide me on my journey toward God? I suspect so.

Of course the dream voice didn't answer my question with a "yes" or "no." I'm not surprised . . . dreams, like good teachers, seem to encourage me to look at issues with a new understanding so I will draw my own conclusions.

☙❧

Later in the night I dreamed:

> I AM DRIVING BEHIND A GREEN AND WHITE GARBAGE TRUCK. A MAN IS STANDING IN THE BACK OF THE TRUCK WHERE THE GARBAGE GOES. THE TRUCK LOOKS CLEAN, BRAND NEW, BUT AS IT TRAVELS SOUTH DOWN THE ROAD TO TOWN, THE BACK STARTS TO CLOSE. THE MAN WHO IS STANDING IN THE BACK YELLS AT ME TO TELL THE DRIVER THAT HE (THE MAN) IS STILL IN THERE. I ACCELERATE TO HURRY AROUND THE TRUCK TO TELL THE DRIVER, AND HE PULLS OVER. THE DRIVER IS SAYING SOMETHING TO ME, BUT HE DOESN'T SEEM VERY ALARMED. HE PULLS TO THE LEFT SIDE OF THE ROAD. I PULL IN FRONT OF HIM SO I AM FACING HIM AND THE CURB IS TO MY RIGHT. IT IS THEN THAT I LEARN FROM THE DRIVER THAT A PREGNANT WOMAN IS IN THE BACK TOO, BUT I HADN'T SEEN HER. I DON'T KNOW IF THE PEOPLE IN THE BACK OF THE TRUCK ARE OKAY OR NOT.

In previous dreams, the GARBAGE TRUCK has been a symbol that represents cleaning away old debris and baggage that I don't need any more. But this GARBAGE TRUCK is CLEAN and BRAND NEW, implying that it has a new purpose. The truck is mostly WHITE (holy) with GREEN (growth/healing) trim. The masculine is in the BACK of the TRUCK and the back is open. The DRIVER doesn't seem to know the MAN is back there. *Why* is he back there? Did he climb in? Is he looking for something? And, more importantly, did *I* unknowingly throw out this masculine dream character?

The DRIVER mentions that a PREGNANT WOMAN is in the BACK OF THE TRUCK, and that she is about to give birth. Give birth to what? Or to whom? The fact that the TRUCK is heading in a southern direction indicates that this journey is moving into my outer physical world . . . and, notably, toward my town. What does my movement and that of the DRIVER tell me? . . . Although the DRIVER PULLS TO THE LEFT (inner knowledge), I pull my car (journey) in such a way that it is stopped with the CURB on my RIGHT, which suggests that what I am learning will become manifest in my outer physical world. But *what* is it that I am supposed to be learning here?

The back of the GARBAGE TRUCK is closing, like a trash compactor, as the TRUCK is moving—threatening to squash the couple. Sometimes the death of a dream character, just like expelling waste, can be a good thing, symbolizing a rebirth into a new learning or higher spiritual vision . . . but this scene feels as if it is leading somewhere else.

Does the MAN trying to save the life of the WOMAN symbolize my masculine side protecting my feminine? The theme of my recent dreams has shown me that I have unconsciously thrown her out, ignored her, and banished her from my conscious mind. Is he, as the protector, attempting to get me to save this shadow feminine so that she can give birth to my new life? It's obvious that whatever journey I am on can't be completed without the masculine and feminine working together.

In the dream I do stop the TRUCK. Now the masculine and feminine can work together—get back in sync. But the dream doesn't reveal the fate of the MAN and the WOMAN. It appears that I will have to wait for future dreams to find out.

༒

The Divine seems to assign masculine or feminine traits to dream characters and symbols. I am becoming aware that the masculine characters are logical and practical, setting the pace with statements that seem to say "slow down, you can't rush spiritual service and gifts." They call me to action, whereas the feminine characters exhibit passionate, creative, and supportive traits.

This dream really solidifies my understanding of how I have always depended on the masculine side to take control in order to survive emotionally. Whether it was because of Dad's drinking when growing up, or the emotional struggles of working with abused children, or the troubles in my marriage, the masculine took charge. My feeling, feminine side was unable to deal with the fears about being abandoned, or the suffering of the children, or the loneliness.

༒

While doing the dreamwork today, I thought of how panicked I felt when confronted with the possibility of the masculine/feminine and the new life being squashed in the GARBAGE TRUCK. Because of my tendency to have panic attacks, I decided to meditate with the hope of understanding where that feeling comes from. What I realized is that while growing up I became hyperaware of my environment, especially at night, in order to be prepared for any shifts in the family dynamic. Certain situations were perceived as dangerous, and I was terrified of being abandoned and left to fend for myself. I'm sure there is a lingering, unconscious need for me to be in control, to be hyperaware, because of this. My experiences allow me to empathize with all of those children who try to maintain control. They know what may happen to them, psychologically and/or physically, if they don't stay aware.

The meditation also helped me understand why I had those panic attacks on family car trips: because I felt out of control in unfamiliar surroundings! It's that same panicky feeling I get when in crowds—where it's impossible to be hyperaware—and when I ride in the back seat of a car. The reason that the panic attacks are worse at night has to be because sleep represents a significant loss of awareness and control.

The panic attacks go hand in hand with the other problem behaviors I developed in childhood. My behavior in the BIG MAN IN THE WHITE T-SHIRT dream is a perfect example: becoming furious when I couldn't control him. My behavior bordered on bullying. I also employed my "turn away, leave, and ignore" move, my classic response to any hurtful or frustrating situation. Again, this is a way to stay in control. The resulting problem, however, is that it is a form of manipulation, and since childhood it has done nothing but leave problems unresolved and destructive patterns thriving in my relationships.

Now I understand that the work to be done is to become balanced—to restore myself to the healthy, whole person God intended me to be. I need to learn to feel what normal feelings *are* for a given situation, to stay aware of where panic attacks come from and know that that response is no longer needed. Ultimately, I have to realize that I'm *not* in control and that it's okay—God is! I need to awaken my feminine self and trust her to help me let go so I can feel safe in the palm of His hand. Again, the message from the Holy Spirit is *"Do NOT BE AFRAID."*

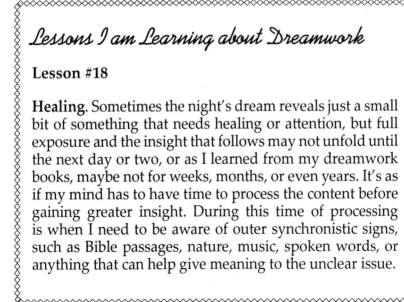

### *Lessons I am Learning about Dreamwork*

**Lesson #18**

**Healing.** Sometimes the night's dream reveals just a small bit of something that needs healing or attention, but full exposure and the insight that follows may not unfold until the next day or two, or as I learned from my dreamwork books, maybe not for weeks, months, or even years. It's as if my mind has to have time to process the content before gaining greater insight. During this time of processing is when I need to be aware of outer synchronistic signs, such as Bible passages, nature, music, spoken words, or anything that can help give meaning to the unclear issue.

*Our spirits were designed by God to
communicate with Deity.*
**A.W. Tozer**[1]


*I choose to believe that, from beyond time, a saving
mystery breaks into our time at odd
and unforeseeable moments.*
**Frederick Buechner**[2]


*Jesus began to weep.*
**John 11:35**[3]


*For he works in secret, and he will be perceived,
and his appearing will be very sudden.*
**Julian of Norwich**[4]

Chapter 13

# Where Are You, Jesus?

Dream: *Colorado Semis;* Vision: *The Hanging Jesus*

## March 8, 2007 (continued)

As if all the intensity and learning from the GARBAGE TRUCK dream wasn't enough, I dreamed this afterward:

> I AM AT A TRUCK DEPOT. THERE ARE ABOUT FIVE SEMI-TRUCKS IN THE GARAGE FACING OUT. I AM SUPPOSED TO LUBRICATE THEM, ALTHOUGH I AM NOT SURE HOW TO DO THIS. I ASK A MAN FOR HELP. HE TAKES EACH ONE OUT BY HAND (AS IF THEY ARE SMALLER — TOY SIZE). HE APPLIES THE OIL AND GREASE. I SEE A JACKET OR LIGHTWEIGHT COAT I HAVE MADE WITH TWO HUGE POCKETS ON EITHER SIDE. I TELL HIM THAT EACH POCKET CAN HOLD AN ENTIRE SEMI-TRUCK. THE JACKET IS LYING ON THE COUNTER. I HAVEN'T PUT IT ON YET. SOMEONE QUESTIONS WHAT I AM DOING. THEY WANT TO BE REASSURED THAT I WON'T TAKE THIS BUSINESS OUT OF COLORADO. I SAY, "NO, NO! I AM JUST LUBRICATING IT."

Trucks again! Hmmm . . . the SEMI-TRUCKS are being LUBRICATED/GREASED. I feel as if they symbolize a large project or event and the lubricating is part of the preparation. I had made a JACKET OR LIGHTWEIGHT COAT, possibly indicating spring or fall? Or maybe the COAT is supposed to be a form of protection for me, but only LIGHTWEIGHT protection? Protection from what? The COAT has TWO HUGE POCKETS ON EACH SIDE that can each hold a SEMI-TRUCK—the right pocket (outer life) and the left pocket (spiritual/inner nature). Again here are twin symbols that I don't understand! Am I being asked to do something? The JACKET is still lying on the counter—I haven't put it on yet. This tells me that not only do I not know what it is I am supposed to do, but that it is not yet the right time for it. Perhaps I'm not far enough along in this dream course to yet know these answers.

What does it mean when I am asked not to take this BUSINESS out of COLORADO? I can't think of any literal interpretation of traveling to Colorado, but can see that symbolically Colorado represents God's majestic mountains. In the Bible, mountaintops are places of revelation, of spiritual contact with God. I feel as if I am being asked to keep the dreamwork (BUSINESS), in a spiritual place (COLORADO). So, when SOMEONE questions what I am doing, my reply represents reassurance that I will continue to keep a spiritual/religious focus. So far I am simply LUBRICATING the TRUCKS. Whatever they represent, I am evidently getting them ready so they will run smoothly when the time comes. The maintenance being done before the trip is to help the journey flow. Though I don't fully understand what is unfolding here, this dream seems to say that it is all happening as it should.

Is all of this dreamwork leading to some outer activity other than merely doing it for my own insight, growth, and healing? If so, what is it? Until now I had been thinking that the journey was simply my new daily dreamwork adventure. But this dream seems to be preparing me for an outer event or project or journey. Will I eventually be shown what it is? Will I recognize it if something more is being asked of me?

∽∾

It is evening now. Today I learned the importance and the impact of asking Spirit a question before going to sleep, because the mystical answer given in the dreams that follow can give further insight into the themes running through my dreams.

The Holy Spirit has a special way of preparing me for new learning. It is an inner preparation, an inner adjustment, which changes the way I perceive what is true. This process is becoming more and more evident as I observe the patterns in my dreams. The Holy Spirit introduces an issue in a dream that needs attention. But it may take two or three days— maybe longer—before I am fully aware of the significance or impact of the issue.

This makes me think of the story of Saul from the Bible: after Saul had his encounter with Christ on the road to Damascus, he had to sit for three days in blindness before Ananias could heal him, allowing the scales to fall from his eyes. Then he could *see* and he could become the new Paul. Saul needed time to repent, process, reflect, and make sense of what was a dramatic shift in his thinking and his life. The same goes for me!

A few days ago, in the *J.C. PENNEY* dream, the content focused on my difficulties dealing with issues at the children's protective service agency. The next several dreams further addressed the separation and repression of my feminine, feeling side. These dreams over several days were my preparation for understanding a *future* event, which happened today.

Early this afternoon, I went to the grocery store. While in line at the checkout counter, a very agitated and angry young woman employee came over to talk to an older clerk who was checking out my groceries. She said she had just witnessed a mother beating her children. The young employee said she had gone to her supervisor for help but was told that she, the employee, should have said something to the mother. The animated young woman said, "And what, get beat myself?" She started to cry. She was angry with the customer and now angry with her supervisor, not to mention upset that no one intervened to help the children. Still crying, she walked away to repeat her story to another employee.

As I looked around and listened to see if I could see or hear the abusive mother, I didn't hear any crying children, so I suspected that they had already left the store. Wondering what to do and because of my work history, I wanted to help the clerk, give advice, do *something*. This had been my professional life for twenty-two years, for goodness sake! But, thinking that the administration must have its own policy, I decided to do nothing—to just take my groceries and go home.

As I walked out, the scenario kept playing in my mind. I identified with all three roles: the angry and frustrated parent in need of help and relief; the frustrated and helpless witness; and the administrator limited by policy or by fear of interfering in someone else's personal business.

As I pulled out of the store's rainy parking lot and turned the windshield wipers on, I felt my eyes burning and tears rolled down my cheeks! I had faced hundreds, maybe thousands, of situations like this and had never shed a tear. What was different this time?

∾

In my prayers early this morning, I asked Jesus why he hadn't appeared in any of my dreams. Or, had he shown up as one of the dream helpers and maybe I just hadn't recognized him? After I came home from the grocery store I lay down to rest. After waking from my nap, I sat quietly on my bed and asked the Divine "to show me something about God that I have forgotten." I don't know why I said it in quite that way, but those were my exact words. I made my mind blank and suddenly, a vivid image filled the void.

*JESUS IS HANGING UP HIGH, NOT ON A CROSS, BUT AS IF HE HAS ACTUALLY BEEN HANGED. I SEE NO ROPE AND NO ARMS OR HANDS. INSIDE HIS BRILLIANT RED CAPE HE WEARS A LUMINOUS WHITE TUNIC THAT IS COVERED IN BLOOD DOWN THE FRONT. I CAN'T SEE HIS HEAD OR FACE AT FIRST. HE DANGLES . . . EVER SO SLOWLY, TURNING CLOCKWISE. AS THE FRONT OF HIM COMES AROUND, I KNOW I DON'T WANT TO "SEE." I FEEL AS IF I AM A SMALL, FRIGHTENED CHILD. I HIDE BEHIND A PARTIAL WALL — EVEN ONCE DUCKING COMPLETELY*

BEHIND THE WALL. I DON'T WANT TO LOOK, BUT I DO . . . I HAVE TO LOOK. BRIGHT RED BLOOD STAINS THE FRONT OF HIS TUNIC, AND HIS CHEST APPEARS TO BE CAVED IN, AS IF HIS HEART HAS BEEN CUT OUT. THE SAME IS TRUE OF HIS EYES, NOSE, EARS, AND MOUTH . . . THEY AREN'T THERE. JUST THIS BLOODY MESS.

As horrifying as it was to see the lifeless, bloody figure hanging and slowly turning, my soul wanted to take the image in. I was awake! I was conscious, and was being given something quite out of the realm and experience of my usual dreams. I felt as if I needed to give this vision some time, so the dreamwork on it wasn't done right away. Over the next few hours I just let it be.

❧

Now that I feel a bit steadier, I'm ready to work the vision out as if it were a dream. My first thought is, "What have I done?" Like all the abused and neglected children I have worked with, who feel as though they are to blame for the abuse they receive, I feel in some way responsible for this hanging figure's bloody death. I don't want to believe that, but I am a sinner. The sinner in me has done some awful things for which I have prayed and asked for forgiveness. Have my transgressions caused this pain to Jesus?

As I go over the vision in my mind, I see the figure is wearing brown shoes—not Hebrew sandals, but shoes similar to the ones I wear . . . *Aha!* The image represents Jesus *and* me! The "me" who worked in such a difficult job, the "me" who had learned to subdue the feeling, feminine side as a child and had to unconsciously continue to suppress it in order to perform at work.

Not only does Christ understand the pain of those years, he experienced them with me! He is hanging there, dangling, by himself. His senses and his heart have been cut out by the unbearable pain. Just as mine were! As a caseworker I suppressed the unbelievable, gut-wrenching anguish that came from witnessing the terror that adults inflicted on children I continued to suppress it as a supervisor, to protect myself while listening to the heart-breaking real-life stories day after day.

And I know now, in this moment, that this horrifying but awesome image is a *gift* to me—a gift to express and give voice to, in symbolic form, the pain I endured below the level of consciousness during my years at work, and perhaps also in my childhood, when I first learned to shut down my feeling side.

Continuing on this theme, I think I now see additional symbolism in the TRAIN WRECK dream from the other night. In the dream, the train fell over again and again, with the sound gradually separating and diminishing. Perhaps the separation of the loud, thunderous sound from the action is symbolic of how my feelings had to be separated, suppressed from the difficult situations presented to me.

The TRAIN WRECK dream also reminds me of how I felt comforted when realizing the WRECK was choreographed. The dreamwork revealed that I might experience something in the future that at first would feel off-track, but that I should understand that it was staged to help me with my journey. I believe this HANGING-JESUS vision is that staged event.

Without having experienced the dreams and done the dreamwork of the past few days, I would be tempted to see this powerful and emotionally-stirring vision only as a representation of the Judeo-Christian story: that Jesus died for my sins. I might also be tempted to worry that dreamwork might cause me to lose my Christian faith and Christ in the process, as if this dreamwork could be killing off Christ! Not so. The heads-up I received from the choreographed TRAIN WRECK dream prepared me to not overreact to this image, and to look deeper at what other meanings it may continue to reveal. The gift of the image has brought a deep sense of revelation, mercy, and love. I'm closer to Christ than I ever have before. Awed. Touched. Healed.

☙❧

What an incredible day's worth of dreamwork, insight, and healing! As this dreamwork was being finished, I remembered something significant: While in second grade, my friend Margaret came to stay overnight. When her dad came to pick her up in the morning, Mom and I couldn't find her. We finally found her hiding in my closet because she didn't want to go home with her father—she told us he had been hitting her. I'm sure that Mom just didn't know what to do, so she told Margaret that she *had* to go home. After she left, I cried for her pain, and for the helplessness Mom and I felt . . . I did know what the appropriate emotional response was once upon a time.

With the help of the Trinity and the dreamwork, I am going through the difficult process of re-learning how to feel, and the fact that my feeling, empathetic side responded normally at the grocery store this morning is progress! Tears were the appropriate response to learning of the violence experienced by those children and the frustration we all felt at not being able to help them. It was the *normal*, human response I had not allowed myself to experience or express during all of those years at the agency.

My ability to "feel" is becoming conscious and alive—I feel renewed! Even if I slip back into my non-feeling, stoic self in future emotional situations, I know that my dreams and the Holy Spirit will help me to recognize it.

*Lessons I am Learning about Dreamwork*

**Lesson #19**

**Ask.** Ask a question. Pay attention. The Holy Spirit will answer. If the answer is in the form of a dream or vision with a luminous, awe-inspiring symbol, I should not fail to ask, "What part of *me* does this represent?"—even if the symbol appears to be Jesus himself.

*We can tell more about God through the words of a
story than through any amount of theology.*
**Madeleine L'Engle**[1]


*And now, my children, listen to me:
happy are those who keep my ways.
Hear instruction and be wise, and do not neglect it.
Happy is the one who listens to me,
watching daily at my gates,
waiting beside my doors.
For whoever finds me finds life
and obtains favor from the Lord.*
**Proverbs 8:32-35**[2]


*To say that I was born again,
to use that traditional phrase, is to say too much
because I remained in most ways as self-centered and
squeamish after the fact as I was before, and,
God knows, remain so still.
And in another way to say that I was born again is
to say too little because there have been more than a
few such moments since, times from when beyond time
something too precious to tell has glinted in the dusk,
always just out of reach, like fireflies.*
**Frederick Buechner**[3]

Chapter 14

# Restoring the Balance

Dreams: *Fixing the Train; Adrian and the Pink and White Shirt;
An Old Indian; Guarding the Restaurant*

## March 9, 2007

The vision of the HANGING-JESUS is still working on me, although I feel I have come to some relevant insights about it. Still, when the image appears in my mind's eye . . . I can't help wonder what else it might be trying to tell me.

In looking back through my dreamwork this morning, I marveled at the gentle way the dreams have shown me symbols to help me address my inability to get in touch with my suppressed emotions and feelings. The disconnected TREADMILL, the TOASTER that only toasts on one side, the FOSTER CHILD on the roof, the TRAIN WRECK disconnecting from its sound, and the man in the DIRECTOR'S CHAIR who didn't find the chair uncomfortable are all symbols that really hit home.

Then yesterday I had the GARBAGE TRUCK dream, which left the fate of the masculine and feminine unknown . . . *Can* I create a healthy wholeness within me by balancing my masculine and feminine sides? Understanding how I learned to suppress my feeling side as a way of coping with Dad's drinking, the uncertainty of family life, and the pain I saw at work is new to me. Is there more?

I think of Mom, and how she herself was distanced from her feeling side. Her sad and painful experiences as a teenager led to a shutdown of her own feminine feeling side so she could cope. The subconscious suppression of her feelings left her disconnected, which affected her future behavior, reactions, and relationships. As an adult, she dealt silently with Dad's nightly drinking for *twenty-five years*. The alcohol disconnected him; the suppression of her feelings disconnected her . . . did they bequeath their inner and outer dysfunction to me?

❧☙

From a middle-of-the-night dream last night, I remember this brief image:

> I AM PUTTING THE NOSE (FRONT PIECE) BACK ON THE TRAIN, WHICH IS MOVING.

Is this an attempt to restore the senses? Making it possible to continue the journey? Then:

> ADRIAN IS GETTING READY TO GO SOMEWHERE AND NEEDS THE RIGHT CLOTHES. I ACCOMPANY HIM TO THE STORE. HE IS DRESSED IN A SUIT AND LOOKS NICE. I LOOK DOWN AND SEE THAT I HAVE ON WHITE SLIPPERS AND CASUAL CLOTHES. AS WE ENTER THE DOOR OF THE STORE, I SAY TO ADRIAN, "IF MY DAD SEES ME, HE WILL BE UPSET THAT I'M NOT DRESSED UP LIKE YOU ARE."

Adrian is GETTING READY for our journey and needs THE RIGHT CLOTHES. Symbolically, I think Adrian is now my masculine aspect, my protector and encourager from the GARBAGE TRUCK dream and he is continuing with me on my spiritual journey. In this dream, the usual three-figure dynamic—my dreamself plus the masculine and feminine characters—is missing. It is significant that there are just two dream figures. My dreamself *is* the feminine, and Adrian is the masculine!

This dream seems to be continuing the integration of the masculine and feminine. We are shopping for clothes together, but it can't be dress-up clothes (traditional religion) we are in search of, because the masculine is already wearing a *SUIT*. He is dressed formally and looks NICE. Nor is it casual clothes we are after, because I have on CASUAL CLOTHES and WHITE SLIPPERS, which represent a warm, holy, informal, and comfortable spirituality (non-traditional spirituality). So, what is it that we need for this journey?

Oh, the baggage... "*IF MY DAD SEES ME, HE WILL BE UPSET THAT I'M NOT DRESSED UP LIKE YOU ARE.*" My first reaction is to think that Dad would be critical of my informal path, and I'm wondering if he is warning me. But after I re-read the statement the "if" implies that I am simply revisiting the guilt felt after he reacted the way he did when I started asking questions about our Catholic faith as a teenager. He, the most important masculine figure of my childhood, *squashed* my first attempt at spiritual exploration!

The dream continued:

> WE PROCEED TO THE CLOTHING SECTION—HE GOES TO THE RIGHT AND I GO TO THE LEFT—BUT WE BOTH GET THERE, ARRIVING AT THE SAME PLACE.

Adrian chooses the path to the RIGHT, or outer way, which makes sense since he is quite comfortable with our traditional Lutheran life and spirituality. My dreamself goes to the LEFT, which certainly represents the inner or mystical path I am on now. But, we end up together at the SAME PLACE in the store at a table of shirts.

> WE LOOK FOR AN EXTRA-LARGE SHIRT FOR HIM. I PULL UP A WHITE SHIRT, A PULLOVER TRIMMED IN PINK. I THINK IT MIGHT BE TOO FEMININE, BUT THEN I SEE THAT ADRIAN HAS PULLED UP THE IDENTICAL SHIRT—WE ARE BOTH LIFTING THE SHIRTS UP. I SHOW HIM THE SIZE AND WIDTH AND SAY, "DO YOU THINK THIS IS BIG ENOUGH?"

Not only do we arrive in the same place despite taking separate paths, but we also choose the same SHIRT! It is A PULLOVER (informal), WHITE (holy and masculine) and has PINK TRIM (love and feminine). We LIFT THEM UP as if asking for a blessing and for approval from each other. When I realize we have both selected the very same SHIRT, I feel such joy and happiness!

When I show Adrian the SIZE AND WIDTH (extra-large—his actual size), and say, "DO YOU THINK THIS IS BIG ENOUGH," I believe that my feminine is expressing belief and trust in my masculine's ability to protect and care for her. She doesn't have to be afraid of expressing feelings anymore because he has also chosen the IDENTICAL SHIRT trimmed in pink—the color of love and a symbol that the masculine and feminine are clearly working together. The SHIRT itself is the symbol of a holy garment of love that provides restoration and protection of the heart, the heart that, like Jesus' in the vision, was absent for so much of my life.

The healing that comes from these dreams amazes me! The *STORE* in the dream is the one where, yesterday, I listened to that young store clerk agonize over the abusive mother! In this dream, the Holy Spirit takes the *outer* symbol of the *STORE* from yesterday—a place of pain— and within that location heals my *inner* pain caused by the separation from my feminine, feeling side. This is how stories can heal. The Divine provides a renewal, a new definition for an old symbol; God restores the heart.

ॐ

In my third dream this morning, the Native American theme resurfaces.

> BACK IN THE APARTMENT BUILDING *I* AM
> EXCITED TO FIND OUT THAT AN OLD *NATIVE*
> *AMERICAN* MAN LIVES THERE. *I* HOPE TO
> MEET HIM.

A literal explanation for this segment may be my excitement about Marcy joining our Bible study group. I am looking forward to the new symbolism and ideas that her Native American roots will add to our discussions. The fact that the Native American symbol in the dream is a man is surely a projection of myself, because I assume that if I were going through the difficult life challenges that Marcy is going through right now, my feeling side would shut down. In truth, this is not the case—she is very in touch with her feminine, feeling side. Does this segment mean that I am becoming more aware of when I feel the need to shift out of the "feeling" mode?

In the fourth dream:

> I HAVE BEEN INVITED BY THE OWNER OF A
> RESTAURANT TO STAY OVERNIGHT. I TELL HER
> THAT SHE DOESN'T HAVE TO MAKE UP A BED.
> MY FRIEND COMES THROUGH THE DOOR AND
> SAYS, "CANDY CAN SLEEP ON THE COUCH." WE
> ARE THERE FOR A REASON, PERHAPS TO GUARD
> THE RESTAURANT. IT SEEMS THAT WE HAVE
> BEEN ASKED BY THE OWNER TO DO THAT.

A RESTAURANT or STORE represents a place of choices of nourishment or spiritual offerings. The STORE in the PINK AND WHITE SHIRT dream is really a "mega store," a place that has many items, including clothes and food. The SHIRT that my masculine and feminine choose in the dream protects the heart and chest area of the body. Now the RESTAURANT food will nourish that body and feed the senses that were absent in the TRAIN WRECK dream, and CUT OUT in the HANGING-JESUS vision.

This dream, like the two other RESTAURANT dreams earlier this month, hints again at an invitation to partake in and enjoy other spiritual disciplines . . . but I think it goes even further than that. In the first dream, I walked by the restaurant not sure that I wanted to go in, which I took to mean I was not yet open to new spiritual experiences. In the second dream, I went into the restaurant but wondered about the less-than-well-done TILAPIA, which still showed my reluctance to take in spiritual change.

Now in this RESTAURANT dream, I am actually *guarding* the restaurant—guarding the gift of exploring other realms of spirituality! Through this dream and through this month's dreamwork, the Holy Spirit has shown me that it is possible to sample different spiritual disciplines and that by doing so, the foundation of my Christian faith will only get stronger. Many of the spiritual readings I have been exploring interweave with my dreams and the quotes and passages I have found most pertinent reinforce the validity and importance of this new spiritual journey. I am hungry for more!

*Lessons I am Learning about Dreamwork*

**Lesson #20**

**Details.** When interpreting dreams, pay attention to the details—in the dream and in the dream notes. Details can help understand patterns and connections, which can lead to incredible insight and guidance.

# PART V

# COMPASSION

# AND

# GROWTH

*Dream images that reflect the complexities of the self may be ambiguous, seemingly trivial and banal, or even disturbing and distressing on first encounter, but at some deep level or another, like the magic mirror, they always speak truth.*

**Jeremy Taylor**[1]

*Send her forth from the holy heavens, and from the throne of your glory send her that she may labor at my side, and that I may learn what is pleasing to you. For she knows and understands all things and she will guide me wisely in my actions and guard me with her glory.*

**Wisdom of Solomon 9:10-11**[2]

*Truth is within ourselves; it takes no rise
From outward things, whate'er you may believe,
There is an inmost centre in us all,
Where truth abides in fullness; and around,
Wall upon wall, the gross flesh hems it in,
This perfect, clear perception—which is truth.
A baffling and perverting carnal mesh
Binds it, and makes all error: and to know
Rather consists in opening out a way
Whence the imprisoned splendour may escape,
Than in effecting entry for a light
Supposed to be without.*

**Robert Browning**[3]

Chapter 15

# Finding Feminine Wisdom

Dreams: *Puffy Eyes; The Way of Sophia/Holding Back*

**March 11, 2007**

All of the excitement about these dreams has been waking me up in the middle of the night, so last night I decided to take half of a sleeping pill to see if it would help me stay asleep until the morning dream. It didn't work! Instead, I woke up in the middle of the night after this short dream:

> A LITTLE "BLACK" GIRL HAS SCRATCHES ON HER EYES. SHE HAS PUFFY EYES, LIKE THE FIGHTER IN THE BOXING MATCH MOVIE LAST NIGHT. SHE IS ENTERING AN ARENA THROUGH A CORRIDOR ALL BY HERSELF, AND I REALIZE SHE PROBABLY CAN'T SEE.

This one is not hard to get! *I* am that LITTLE GIRL. The fact that the image of the girl appears in BLACK and the implied blindness suggest that I need to address something about myself. The dream incorporates images from the boxer movie Adrian and I watched last night to show me the puffiness of my eyes and the heaviness they feel from the sleeping pill. My dreamself is ENTERING AN ARENA, or the theatre of dreams, through a CORRIDOR—a narrow path—ALL BY HERSELF, without helpers. Usually there are several characters and helpers in the dreams, but in this short segment I am alone and unable to SEE. This strong message says that even though the pill might make me sleepier, it might also impair the dreamwork process!

My next dream reiterates the same message:

> THERE IS A WOMAN FRIEND WITH ME IN THE CAR. WE ARE GOING TO A MUSIC RECITAL. WE DRIVE BY A FRIEND'S HOUSE, AND I SEE SOMEONE ON THE FRONT PORCH. AT FIRST I THINK IT MIGHT BE MY FRIEND WHO LIVES THERE, BUT THEN I SEE THAT IT IS HER DAUGHTER. SHE IS SITTING IN A CHAIR WITH HER HEAD BACK. HER FACE LOOKS PUFFY. I COMMENT THAT SHE LOOKS "HIGH."

> WE TURN RIGHT ONTO A ROCKY, BUMPY ROAD. I SEE A CAR HEADING OUR WAY ON MY SIDE OF THE ROAD. I FIGURE THEY WILL MOVE OVER SINCE THEY ARE GOING SLOW TOO.

The young woman ON THE FRONT PORCH is really Cassie. I know how she has struggled with addiction! She represents the drowsy feeling from the sleeping pill. Her HEAD BACK implies heading backward as opposed to heading forward, and, again, tells me that the pills are not helpful for dreamwork.

The FRIEND in the CAR and I TURN RIGHT (outer). The direction we are going is north (spiritual) onto a ROCKY, BUMPY ROAD. The path is difficult, with big rocks and weeds—a road that has not been used in a long time— perhaps an obsolete path. Or maybe the dream suggests that it *should* be obsolete. A CAR is coming in my direction but going . . . so . . . s..l..o..w that I am not worried about a collision. My only concern is that the way of travel is very SLOW. These images refer to my decision to take that pill! But, I also see a spiritual aspect to the dream's message:

> I TELL THE FRIEND/HELPER I PROBABLY HAVEN'T TAKEN THE BEST ROAD. THE WOMAN INDICATES SHE USED TO KNOW ANOTHER WAY BUT ISN'T SURE OF IT. I SAY THERE MIGHT BE A CROSSROAD OVER INTERSTATE 75. SHE SAYS "YES, THE ROAD IS CALLED SOPHIA, AND THEN YOU TURN RIGHT ON A ROAD THAT PARALLELS 75 TO THE MUSIC STUDIO." I SAY, "YOU DO KNOW HOW TO GET THERE!" I WONDER WHY SHE HADN'T GUIDED ME THERE, OR TOLD ME WHERE TO TURN, SO WE WOULDN'T HAVE HAD TO GO ON THIS INCREDIBLY BUMPY ROAD.

Just as in the dream of the TWO BUILDINGS divided by a RAVINE, there are two parallel paths. Here they are elevated on either side of a busy INTERSTATE. We are heading north, into higher consciousness or into the dream world. The road on the right is BUMPY and difficult to follow, just as is true of the BUILDING ON THE RIGHT OF THE RAVINE in my other dream. It seems that A BUMPY, ROCKY, ROAD is my dream image for a direction or path that will not be helpful for me. Being placed on my RIGHT tells me that this symbol is referring to something in my outer life—in this case, the sleeping pill. My companion indicates that she knows another way, but, for some reason, she *holds back*. She acts as if she is not sure, because she wants *me* to remember instead of answering for me. It's that familiar behavior again—the dream helper holding back and encouraging me to find my *own* way.

⌒∂∼⌒

The name SOPHIA is unknown to me. The internet was used first, then I looked it up in some of my books. It was found in the Bible, Proverbs 8 is about Sophia and that she is Wisdom! Sophia is also referred to in Psalms, the Apocryphal Wisdom of Solomon, and the New Testament. Once again, I am in awe of the dream process—SOPHIA refers to the feminine aspect of God!

In another book, I found this interesting quote by Aristotle:

> *Man is in a privileged position: his human soul has the divine gift of intellect, which makes him kin to God and a partaker in the divine nature. This godly capacity of reason puts him above plants and animals. As body and soul, however, man is a microcosm of the whole universe, containing within himself its basest materials as well as the divine attribute of reason. It is his duty to become immortal and divine by purifying his intellect. Wisdom (sophia) was the highest of all the human virtues; it was expressed in contemplation (theoria) of philosophical truth which, as in Plato, makes us divine by imitating the activity of God himself. Theoria was not achieved by logic alone, but was a disciplined intuition resulting in an ecstatic self-transcendence. Very few people are capable of this wisdom, however, and most can achieve only phronesis, the exercise of foresight and intelligence in daily life.[4]*

Is dreamwork part of the "disciplined intuition" path? Is it the feminine path to, as well as the communication tool of the Divine Mystery? Is SOPHIA a new issue for me to explore, in addition to the recent theme of balancing my masculine and feminine aspects? Does learning about SOPHIA mean learning a parallel but equally spiritual path to God in addition to traditional Christianity? It's safe to assume God is Spirit and has no gender, but would thinking of God in feminine terms as well as masculine help my quest to understand the Divine? Does my concept of God need a balancing of the masculine and feminine principles, just as I do? Is there more to be learned about this type of spirituality than just dreamwork?

Just as my childhood imagining of God as an old man with a flowing white beard sitting on a throne in the clouds evolved into a genderless image of the Divine Spirit, I now find myself opening up to the idea that God has a feminine side.

The dream continues:

> ANYWAY, WE MAKE IT TO THE MUSIC STUDIO AND WATCH A PERFORMANCE. IT TURNS OUT THAT I AM SINGING A VOCAL ACCOMPANIMENT TO A CHRISTMAS HYMN WITH ANOTHER SINGER. WHEN WE FINISH WITH THE "TAKE," I NOTICE THE PIANO ACCOMPANIST HAS LONG RED HAIR AND LOOKS FAMILIAR. SHE SMILES AS IF SHE KNOWS ME. SHE SAYS SOMETHING LIKE, "WELL, CANDY, THIS IS YOUR THIRD TIME PUTTING THIS MUSIC TOGETHER" (OR "YOUR THIRD TIME RECORDING OR ARRANGING"). "YOU'RE GETTING KNOWN AROUND HERE." I REPLY, "WHERE DO I KNOW YOU FROM? COLLEGE? OR HIGH SCHOOL?" SHE SHAKES HER HEAD AND SAYS, "JUST HERE AT THE STUDIO."

"*ANYWAY,*" implies that, in spite of my mistake with the pill, I am still given a dream with which to work. In this section of the dream, there is a performance and a recording going on. Literally, the word *TAKE* implies a performance worthy of a *RECORDING*. It doesn't have to be done over again. Symbolically, I have learned the lesson of the pill and the *BUMPY ROAD*—it "takes."

This is the first time in a dream that I have ever sung a song! It leaves me feeling happy—as if Spirit has affirmed that singing is a spiritual gift.

The *ACCOMPANIST HAS LONG RED HAIR*, representing feminine, passion and vitality. When she says that I am *GETTING KNOWN AROUND HERE*, does she mean in the dream/spiritual world? Or, is this little dream segment hinting at doing something with music in the future? When I ask the *ACCOMPANIST* where I know her from, she replies, "*. . . ONLY AT THE STUDIO*" (the inner dream world). Maybe I have met this lovely helper in other forgotten dreams. In the next dream segment:

> *I AM RIDING IN THE BACK OF A CAR WHERE TIM HAS PLACED ME. WE GO INTO A RESTAURANT AND THEN COME BACK OUT AFTER DINNER. I ASK HIM IF HE STILL WANTS ME TO RIDE IN THE BACK. HE OPENS THE BACK DOOR OF THE CAR. HE IS PLEASANT, SMILING, AND SAYS, "YES." I GET IN. THERE ARE OTHERS IN THE CAR. HE GETS IN THE DRIVER'S SEAT AND PULLS THE CAR OUT OF THE PARKING SPOT. I START TO TELL HIM TO TURN ON HIS LIGHTS (IT IS NIGHT TIME), BUT HE FINALLY DOES SO AS HE TURNS LEFT THROUGH THE PARKING LOT.*

In the dream, Tim clearly wants me behind him. Not in the sense of being in a supportive position, but rather that he has put our marriage, and the issues we had, behind him. As I START TO TELL HIM what to do, TO TURN ON HIS LIGHTS, thinking it will help illuminate his journey, I hold back, and eventually he does it on his own. He has moved on and doesn't need me to enlighten him.

Again, the theme of *holding back* appears. I hold back just as the dream helper did in the WAY OF SOPHIA dream. Also, in the dream the helpers never say it is "wrong" to take sleep aids, or that I am going the "wrong" way, or that holding back from telling Tim to turn on his lights is the "right" thing for me to do. These judgment words don't seem to be helpful to dreamwork. The dream helpers never use these terms—they simply *suggest*. I appreciate their gentle guidance toward correcting my wayward and less-than-helpful behavior. It appears the Holy Spirit may have used the opportunity of my taking the sleep medication to lecture on the theme of temperance . . .

The dream continues:

> LATER, I IMAGINE TAKING THE SOPHIA ROAD, THE SMOOTH ROAD THAT GLIDES OVER INTERSTATE 75, AND PASS WHAT I REMEMBER IS AN INTERESTING CRAFT OR SEWING STORE. I NOW KNOW A "BETTER" WAY TO THE MUSIC STUDIO.

The SOPHIA road is a smoother path over the INTERSTATE 75 corridor of busy night dreaming, rather than the BUMPY ROAD caused by the sleeping pill. This new path, symbolized by the crossroad named SOPHIA, is something that I *do* want to explore. Working through my dreams *is* a creative (CRAFT/SEWING) journey. And, finally, the smooth path—not the bumpy path—to the STUDIO, to the place where I sing and record my dreams, *is* the best way to the "spotlight" dream—the most important dream of the night.

આૠ

It is immensely consoling that the Holy Spirit provides a dream that sends me on an exciting adventure to learn about the concept of SOPHIA—feminine Wisdom—during the very night in which I have been so unwise!

*Lessons I am Learning about Dreamwork*

**Lesson #21**

**Hold Back.** When working in groups or discussing dreams with individuals, share dreams, visions, and symbols, but, like the dream helpers, allow others to draw their own conclusions, as they are on their own path and must discover their own answers.

**Lesson #22**

**Non-Judgmental Language.** When doing dreamwork, stay away from judgmental language, such as the words "right" and "wrong." It is more helpful to use "better," "best," or "not the best." This allows the dreamwork process to be one of gentle guidance, not of judgment and punishment.

*Creation is so endlessly complex and so intricately
interconnected that if we are not very careful and
deeply reverent before what is clearly way beyond us,
no matter how well-intentioned we are,
we will probably interfere,
usually in a damaging way,
with what God has done and is doing.
So begin by not doing anything: attend, adore.*
**Eugene H. Peterson**[1]

*Do not be conformed to this world,
but be transformed by the renewing of your minds, so
that you may discern what is the will of God—what is
good and acceptable and perfect.*
**Romans 12:2**[2]

*There are opposite tendencies in us that remain
unconscious and form themselves into another person
inside of ourselves.*
**John Sanford**[3]

*It seems paradoxical, but eminently satisfactory,
that it is only through knowing oneself extremely well
that one can find a way to self-forgetfulness.*
**Sara Maitland**[4]

Chapter 16

# Black and White Thinking

Dreams: *Reconciliation/Invasive Vine;*
*The Administrator/Nun; Slick Willy*

**March 14, 2007**

Ever since this dream process started, I have been afraid that a dream will be critical of me; that it will show me that I've done something wrong. Sometimes I feel like a child, who's afraid to be told that she's "been a bad girl."

Because of this (lifelong!) fear of criticism, there is a concern that it may lead me to misinterpret dream symbols . . . Am I so afraid of disappointing God that I expect to be admonished and chastised in my dreams? And does this, in turn, color and skew my interpretations? Perhaps that is why the Holy Spirit has repeated so many times in my dreams, "God loves you: don't be afraid!" I need to remember that.

❧❧

Upon waking I wrote down my first dream this morning and realized that I couldn't remember a part of the dream. It's a longer dream with four scenes, the second of which escapes me. The three segments I do remember seem to take me on a circular path that corresponds to the Crossroads/Quadrants Map. Segments one and two are in the upper half of the circle and represent the more spiritual part of the night's dream, but my recollection is only of scene one:

> I AM GOING DANCING WITH SOMEONE. RAY, THE LOCAL GAS STATION OWNER, IS THE DANCE INSTRUCTOR. I'M NOT SURE WE WILL GET TO DANCE, THOUGH I REALLY WANT TO, BUT . . .

The dream leaves off with my sensing that someone needs my help. But who? Hmmm. I just can't remember the second segment. It is a blank, and it is in the most spiritual quadrant . . .

The third segment:

> As I WALK IN A GARDEN, I REACH DOWN TO PULL A WEED, WHICH IS A VINE. A DREAM FRIEND SAYS, "THANKS, THOSE ARE SO INVASIVE!"

It is not a vine from "I am the vine, you are the branches." It's one of those nasty pea-vines that smother and suffocate other plants. What does this INVASIVE VINE represent?

Now I have three puzzles: 1) Not being able to DANCE until I do something else; 2) The need to remember a more spiritual part of the dream; and 3) I start to PULL an INVASIVE WEED. But why?

Ray used to provide the gas for my car (journey) and would fix it when it broke down . . . is something broken that needs fixing? I really want to dance in this dance hall, but evidently there is something that needs to be done first.

As my mind wanders over the blank part of the dream, trying to pull it into consciousness, it seems I am intentionally being prevented access. I also know that it is important to understand why. Maybe the answer is in the third segment where I start to PULL THE WEED from the garden. What does the WEED represent? It might be an initial image of the problem—something INVASIVE that needs to be pulled out. But what?

If all of these dream segments really do fit on my Crossroads/Quadrants Map, then the fourth segment of the dream is located in the quadrant that corresponds to my outer world:

> I AM VISITING MY FRIEND AT HER APARTMENT. SHE HAS A BROOM AND IS SWEEPING OUTSIDE HER PART OF THE BUILDING. I HAVE A DOUBLE PUSH BROOM, AND I AM TRYING TO PUSH IT THROUGH THE BUSHES AND ONTO HER SIDEWALK. SHE SHOWS ME HOW TO COME AROUND TO THE PAVED PATH BY THE GARAGE.

Who is this friend? What do the images of the BROOMS mean? Why is mine a DOUBLE PUSH BROOM? As I list these questions, I am puzzled without any answers.

❧❦

These earlier segments are too confusing to me, so I am going to work on the next dream that I remember from last night:

> I AM EATING AT A TABLE. THE TABLE TURNS INTO A PLACE TO WASH UP, AND I BEGIN WASHING MY HANDS. GLEN COMES OUT WEARING A NUN'S

HABIT. HE IS TALKING TO ANOTHER MAN. I
HURRY TO GET OUT OF THEIR WAY. AS I SOAP
MY HANDS UP WITH WHITE SOAP, I CAN SMELL
ON THEM THE DINNER I JUST ATE. AT FIRST
IT IS A GOOD AROMA. THEN I AM AFRAID THE
SMELL IS MAKING ME SICK, SO I KEEP WASHING.
THEN I AM UNDER THE TABLE, CLOSE TO THE
CARPETED FLOOR, BETWEEN THE TABLE LEGS.

I STAND UP AND SAY "HI" TO GLEN. I ASK HIM
WHAT IS GOING ON. HE ASKS IF I REMEMBER
PUBLIC LAW 42-418, OR SOME NUMBER
LIKE THAT, WHICH GOVERNS EDUCATION.
I HESITATE. I REMEMBER THAT TIM USED
TO TALK ABOUT LAWS THAT GOVERN THE
TEACHING OF HANDICAPPED CHILDREN, BUT
I DON'T MENTION THAT. GLEN CONTINUES:
"WELL, THIS LAW TELLS ABOUT WHAT CAN AND
CANNOT BE TAUGHT." HE IS TALKING TO ME AS
IF I KNOW WHAT HE IS TALKING ABOUT, BUT I
AM A SOCIAL WORKER, NOT AN EDUCATOR.

Then, as I was waking:

I HEAR A BASEBALL PLAYER TALKING ABOUT
SOMEONE THROWING A BALL OFF BASE, OR
BEING OFF BASE.

This second dream has me stumped and frustrated
as I was with the first dream! At work, GLEN was always
sharing things that were over my head. He treated
me as someone important and sincerely thought I
would understand what he was saying, but I always
struggled to comprehend the information. My fear of
being criticized, and my continuous worry that I would

be viewed less favorably, kept me from admitting my ignorance and confusion.

Now I am having the same problem with these dreams! My dreamself struggles to understand Glen in the dream, and now I'm having trouble figuring out the meaning of the dream.

❧❧

It's evening. I gave up on dreamwork this morning and went to Bible study. After thinking about the dreams through the rest of the day, their meaning is still puzzling. I am just not able to understand the symbol of the INVASIVE VINE, and the BOSS in the NUN'S HABIT.

To add to the day's frustration, today our computer lost its e-mail system! As I was mulling over the dream symbols in vain, Adrian and I also wrestled for hours and hours to "fix" our e-mail—with no successful results.

Now I have a migraine! This is *not* a good time for me to do dreamwork. I am going to bed.

❧❧

**March 15, 2007**

Last night I took my migraine pills and fell into bed exhausted. I asked God to help me understand the confusing dreams from yesterday morning and to please give me *simple, clear images* that could be understood.

This morning I am feeling better, but the medication has left me feeling spacey. I am back on the couch with my paperwork to figure these dreams out. The dream of this morning might turn out to be helpful, but first I need to work more directly with yesterday's symbols. Now that I'm feeling better, they don't seem as daunting.

So, what does the symbol of the VINE represent? In the dream I am not sure that I am doing the right thing by PULLING OUT THE VINE, but a helper assures me that it is not only a WEED, but also an INVASIVE VINE. In the APARTMENT BUILDING part of the dream, the FRIEND with the BROOM appears to be Natalie. Our relationship has been strained by my pulling back because I disagree with what she has been doing in her personal life . . . Am I supposed to tell her to stop—as in PULL OUT THE VINE? I'm not sure . . . this interpretation doesn't feel right.

I can't believe the synchronicity happening here—as I am thinking these thoughts, the smell of skunk is wafting through the window! Now I *know* I'm not getting the interpretation correct. But at least I am being guided.

My experience with pea vines is that they smother and kill what they latch onto. They take over . . . Am I trying to take over something? Like trying to take control of Natalie's behavior? . . . *Aha!* This is not about me needing to help *Natalie* get rid of the VINE, it's about me needing to pull it from *my* garden—from my heart, which has become smothered with hard feelings against her. The dream helper appears in the form of Natalie to show me that I need to sweep, to clean up my faulty perception, and forgive myself of my own past wrong-doing, so that our relationship can flourish and blossom. Not to correct *her* behavior, but *my own*! This feels right. I need to talk to her, to be a compassionate listener, so our friendship can be renewed—I will definitely call her and make a date for lunch.

⋖⋗

When these four segments are viewed together, I see a kind of warning: It seems I am being told that certain aspects of higher spiritual learning will be blocked from my awareness (I can't go DANCING!) unless I do the necessary work of reconciliation: cleansing, forgiving, healing, etc.

Some dreams, like this one, have a kind of circular nature. Any place I come in on the dream soon circles around to bring in the other parts. Through the four segments, all of the different scenes work together to tell me that the journey to or process of experiencing the Divine requires doing the work and taking the path to *personal wholeness*.

Even though the blank scene is never known, I realize that I can't remember it for a reason, and feel satisfied with my understanding of the dream as a whole.

⋖⋗

Now on to the ADMINISTRATOR/NUN dream!

In this dream I am WASHING AND WASHING MY HANDS WITH WHITE (holy) SOAP as if I can't get them clean enough from handling oily food . . . Glen, (my favorite!) ex-boss, stands next to me wearing a NUN'S habit. As he talks I keep washing my hands. I ask him: "WHAT'S GOING ON?" He asks me if I remember a public law, but because of my fear of being criticized, I don't bring up what I do and do not know about it.

After thinking about the law and calling Tim today to ask him about it, he told me the actual number is 94-142, a former law that governed education. In the dream, Glen says the law is about WHAT CAN AND CANNOT BE TAUGHT (speaking about it as if it were still in effect). When I spoke with Tim, he said that the old law was about *who must* be taught. Of course, as an educational administrator, Glen knows what the law was, but he states it differently in the dream to "educate" me about my judgmental ways, my hard-line views of "right" and "wrong," and my arrogant efforts to "fix" things, spiritual and otherwise, including wanting to give advice to Tim in the HOLDING BACK dream and being critical of Natalie.

For twenty-two years I had to take a hard-line approach because it was required in order for me to do my investigative work and evaluations for the courts. How could this way of thinking *not* seep into other aspects of my life? I'm sure it caused me to rigidly evaluate my own path and judge the people in my life. Having a hard-judging German Catholic background could only have added to the problem! And although Mom and Dad were not harsh with me, I grew up fearing that I would disappoint them, and that childlike fear still lingers in me, making me turn my fear of judgment into judgment of others.

The fact that I am continually WASHING with holy SOAP during the dream emphasizes my quest for perfection and even points to my arrogance in thinking that I know what "perfect" is! But, *I am forgetting that because of Jesus' sacrifice, God already sees me as cleansed*! Because

I am not conscious of this knowledge in the INVASIVE VINE dream, my desire for perfection is projected onto Natalie, judging *her* behavior.

When I tell Glen, "I'm not an EDUCATOR. I'm a SOCIAL WORKER," I am telling him that I am not in the business of teaching and learning; I'm in the business of rescuing and saving . . . *Aha!* I finally "get it"! My approach to Natalie is one of "saving" instead of learning—I need to learn from sorting out my own faulty perceptions and to work toward restoring our relationship. This idea is reinforced at the end of the dream, when I hear a BASEBALL PLAYER TALK ABOUT SOMEONE BEING OFF BASE . . . me, of course.

Whew. I feel lighter now—relieved of more baggage!

⧫

The Holy Spirit's presentation of Glen in a NUN'S HABIT is God's way of saying, "Lighten up, Candy. Stop looking at life strictly in black and white." I also realize that the NUN'S HABIT on an ADMINISTRATOR represents a spiritual twist on an educational law. The actual law affirms that *all* children have the right to an education no matter what their handicapping condition; the twist is that all of God's children *are* handicapped (sinful), yet He loves them all. All can be taught by the Holy Spirit!

In this dream there is yet *another* reference to my health: first, my attempt to wash greasy food from my hands is a reminder of how oily food is unhealthy and that its lingering effects are hard to remove from my body; second, the constant flow of WATER over my hands coincides with the headache I woke with yesterday morning. I've noticed that whenever waking with one, there have been images of large quantities of water in my dreams—perhaps a symbol of what triggers my headaches?

∂∾⟆

The ADMINISTRATOR/NUN dream is so rich with literal and symbolic meaning! Literally, this afternoon I learned that, sadly, Glen has a very serious health problem and has to stay at home while he heals. Janie, who worked with him also, tells me that he doesn't want *any* visits, calls, or cards, etc. It sounds as if he literally wants to be "cloistered." I will pray for him.

Also, at Bible study yesterday, we studied next Sunday's scripture, the Prodigal Son story. I learned from the group discussion that this story is about our loving Father's abundant love for all His children, even the most wayward.

What synchronicity! I am amazed at how my unconscious seemed to know the theme of the scripture reading ahead of time! The dreams that occur on Wednesday morning almost always point to, and are affirmed by, a reading in our Wednesday Bible study; and the Sunday morning dreams are almost always echoed in that day's sermon.

It seems that a willingness and holy intent to be aware of *meaning* in the outer world is matched in like measure by the Holy Spirit's uncanny willingness to affirm and teach.

∂∾⟆

I'm finally ready to work with *this* morning's dream:

*I AM SITTING IN A ROOM WAITING FOR A HEARING. I DON'T KNOW WHAT IT IS ABOUT, BUT I AM ACCOMPANYING A WOMAN FRIEND. A HANDSOME DARK-HAIRED MAN ASKS IF I WILL LOOK AT HIS BOOK, A BOOK OF TRIAL PICTURES. I SAY, "I CAN, BUT I DON'T KNOW ANYTHING ABOUT THIS TRIAL. I AM JUST A VISITOR WITH MY FRIEND." I MOVE OVER TO SIT BY HIM AND REALIZE I AM SITTING ON HIS LAP. I FEEL MY BARE LEG RUB AGAINST HIS BARE LEG. IT IS SENSUOUS BUT NOT A GOOD THING, SO I MOVE BACK TO THE SEAT WHERE I WAS BEFORE. I LOOK AT HIS BOOK. THERE ARE PICTURES OF THE INSIDE OF A PERSON'S HOUSE, WITH KIDS, CLOTHES, AND ROOMS, PAGE AFTER PAGE. I SAY, "I CAN TELL YOU'RE A DEFENSE ATTORNEY. THESE LOOK LIKE A MAGAZINE AD — CLEAN, SANITIZED — THEY RAISE NO ISSUES." HE SMILES AND SHRUGS. I KNOW I AM RIGHT.*

*MY FRIEND AND I MOVE OVER TO ANOTHER COUCH TO GET ANOTHER POINT OF VIEW, AND WE SEE SOME WICKER FURNITURE LIKE A CUPBOARD, A TOILET, AND A COUNTER THAT ARE WORN AND IN NEED OF REPAIR. ALL ARE A DINGY WHITE. I SAY, "HEY! CAN WE USE THAT WHOLE WALL OF STUFF AND PUT IT IN OUR BATHROOM?" I KNOW THE MAN IS LISTENING AND I AM PUTTING ON A SHOW, SWEEPING MY HAND IN AN EXAGGERATED GESTURE FOR EFFECT, TRYING TO GET HIM TO BE CURIOUS*

*AND SELF-CONSCIOUS. MEANWHILE, MY FRIEND*
*REMAINS LAID BACK AND CALM.*

*SHE LAUGHS AS WE REALIZE THE WALL WE*
*HAD JUST SEEN IS NOW IN BACK OF US. I AM*
*ENJOYING HER COMPANY. SHE LEANS BACK*
*AND GETS WHITE PAINT ALL OVER HER. THE*
*WALL OF ITEMS HAS BEEN FRESHLY PAINTED. I*
*GET IT ON ME—AND ALL THE WHILE WE LAUGH*
*AND LAUGH.*

I think "Slick Willy" is an apt name for this DEFENSE
ATTORNEY! Although I don't know what the TRIAL is about,
I know he is not going to present a truthful picture. At first
I feel like a spectator, as if this little drama has nothing to
do with me—I believe the symbols are on trial. But, by
doing the dreamwork, I see Slick Willy as the masculine
part of me who wants me to look good, CLEAN, SANITIZED,
and perfect, as if *I* am the client he is defending. He doesn't
want the outside world to see who I truly am for fear they
will see my flaws, my defects, my humanness, my sins. It
goes along with learning to cover up Dad's alcoholism,
being a "good girl," and hiding from others the wrong
choices I have made. He is awfully compelling, and I
am tempted to go along with this HANDSOME, masculine
fellow (*I FEEL MY BARE LEG RUB AGAINST HIS BARE LEG*), but,
I realize his falseness and align myself with my female
companion instead.

I also see him as the part of me who in outer life asked
God to give me *simple, clear images* in my dreams. But, the
joke is on me! I *am* given simple, clear pictures that LOOK
LIKE A MAGAZINE AD and are CLEAN, SANITIZED—THEY RAISE
NO ISSUES. They may be simple and clear, but they contain

nothing important for me to discover. They do not reveal what I am ultimately searching for: Truth, *God*.

Now sure that Slick Willy is up to no good, my female companion and I move to ANOTHER COUCH (my place for doing dreamwork) so we can see from a different POINT OF VIEW. From there we see a WALL of what appears to be ordinary items. These new symbols are a DINGY WHITE and IN NEED OF REPAIR; their meanings are *not* simple and clear because of the *work* needed to understand them! Suddenly the WALL of dusty WHITE images is behind us, supporting us; but my friend LEANS BACK and gets WHITE PAINT ALL OVER HER and ON ME, and we LAUGH AND LAUGH. Is she laughing because we have seen the light and put one over on old Willy, or could it be for a different reason, like irony?

Unlike my usual self, my FRIEND chooses *not* to be defensive and not to fear criticism. This wonderful female companion puts me at ease and emboldens me to dramatically make a point to Slick Willy—that we are choosing the mysterious, worn and possibly uncomfortable images that reveal the truth, rather than his clean, sanitized images that do not. We align ourselves with the journey that the Holy Spirit provides.

My initial interpretation of the symbols is that a CUPBOARD represents a place to hold *stuff*, like secrets and baggage; a TOILET is a place to get rid of the unnecessary stuff of life, so that I can unlearn in order to grow; and the COUNTER is like my TABLE where life is played out. All of them are WHITE (holy, spiritual) and WORN, IN NEED OF care and REPAIR. Are they worn because they have been well used throughout this intense phase of dreamwork?

Or does the fact that they are IN NEED OF REPAIR tell me I have *more* work to do?

Perhaps this dream is telling me not to be too quick to put Slick Willy on the spot with my EXAGGERATED GESTURES. The ADMINISTRATOR/NUN dream brought to light my fear of being criticized; now, *I* am the one criticizing, or at least embarrassing, part of me (Slick Willy) for his SANITIZED symbols. But, I quickly get my comeuppance when the WHITE PAINT gets on me. The very symbols I have embraced for being mysterious and truthful, "better" than the masculine's, now have fresh, white (holy) paint on them. I could view the white paint as positive—that these symbols are the ones with the true (holy) meanings for me—but it could be negative as well—that the Holy Spirit's obscure symbols of truth can be misinterpreted by our feminine creative self as well as our more rational masculine self and not always lead to Truth if her behavior and intent are not pure, non-judgmental, and Spirit-driven.

The interplay between the masculine and feminine characters in this dream makes me realize that I want to know even more about the combined masculine and feminine aspect of my being. They both have roles to play that are vital to who I am—how I am made by God. Even though I understand more about the masculine and feminine, I have a limited understanding of the Jungian "archetypes." I hope the future dreams explore this area in depth. I know there's more studying for me to do!

୧ৰৎঔ

There is a little more to this dream:

> BACK IN THE WAITING ROOM FOR COURT, I AM
> STANDING, BEING FRIENDLY, AND I SAY, "THIS
> HEARING, THIS CASE, DOESN'T SEEM TO BE A
> BIG DEAL." THE DEFENSE ATTORNEY SMILES AS
> IF HE HAS WON ME OVER. I CONTINUE, "BUT
> THEN, I HAVEN'T SEEN THE OTHER SIDE'S (THE
> PROSECUTOR'S) INFORMATION/ARGUMENT YET."

This part is open-ended and more dreamwork is needed to figure it out: In the dream I am viewing the "other side" as the *prosecution* side. I am pitting both the dream characters and the symbols against each other in a trial. The accurate representation of inner symbols themselves is on trial because of my request to the Holy Spirit to give me simple, clear symbols. (It is as if I am questioning God . . . Whoa!) I am also "prosecuting" poor Slick Willy and his symbols, which leaves me feeling uncomfortable.

Symbols have to be pondered, not prosecuted! I don't have to feel as if I am on trial—God's wisdom is gentle and life- affirming. Learning comes with viewing these dream images from many perspectives. *I need to be aware of my inclination to pigeonhole, to ascribe meaning based on my past experience, instead of letting the dream images speak their fresh truth*!

The imagination of the higher self of my spirit is much more creative and innovative than I could ever imagine. When I learn to trust God, trust the process, do the work required, pray for wisdom, and watch for affirmation, layer upon layer of unneeded walls come down, like peeling an onion. I can let go of the defenses and erroneous thinking that have been blocking my ability to become an integrated, whole person. I can embrace my humanness!

I asked the Holy Spirit to give me symbols that I could understand. Instead, I learned a lesson. She gives exactly what is needed. And, a symbol cannot be squeezed into a definition I come up with if that is not what the symbol means. If the image can't be deciphered after using the dream techniques, I know now to ask the Divine to show me what the message is in another dream or meditation. The Holy Spirit is very patient, kind, firm, and obliging — and She has a wonderful sense of humor. The guidance is steady and true, and though frustration comes with the process at times, I always feel well tended.

*Lessons I am Learning about Dreamwork*

**Lesson #23**

**Circular Dreams.** Often a night's dream contains many themes that are part of a larger, overall theme. This type of dream seems to operate in a circle so the end and beginning can be reached from any starting point. The progression through the scenes comes "full circle" to the start.

**Lesson #24**

**Outer Confirmation.** The outer physical world can confirm the learning of the inner world with synchronistic events. But, if the outer is strangely quiet (no synchronistic or meaningful experiences), or there are "stinky" problems like a skunk in the yard, or the computer crashes, look at the dream again, because the interpretation may be off course.

**Lesson #25**

**Behavior as a Key.** Interpreting my dreamself's behavior may be the key to unfolding the rest of the dream symbols and scenarios.

**Lesson #26**

**Truth.** I can't control a symbol if I really want the *truth*. The Holy Spirit gives me exactly what I need. If I can't decipher a symbol or dream after using dream techniques, I can ask the Holy Spirit to show me what the symbol means in another dream or meditation.

# VI

# GUIDANCE

*One thing seems certain: dreams, daytime encounters,*
*and visions all consist of communications from higher*
*powers who already know much about us and who have*
*a specific purpose in revealing themselves to us and,*
*at least for American Indians,*
*appear in the form of birds and animals.*
**Vine Deloria**[1]

*Therefore I prayed, and understanding was given me;*
*I called on God, and the spirit of wisdom came to me.*
*I do not hide her wealth, for it is an unfailing treasure*
*for mortals, those who get it obtain friendship with God,*
*commended for the gifts that come from instruction.*
**Wisdom of Solomon 7:7 & 13-14**[2]

*Be there, receptive and obedient.*
*Be there praying,*
*"Here I am, the servant of the Lord;*
*let it be with me according to your word" (Luke 1:38).*
**Eugene H. Peterson**[3]

Chapter 17

# *The Question*

Dreams: *Threadbare Brown Couch/Turquoise Band/Cougar Cub;*
*Mohican Marching Orders*


**March 18, 2007**

Because my brain has been full and my head has been
feeling spacey, I haven't been able to remember the dreams
of the last two mornings, which is a good thing! Spirit has
been giving me a break.

❧

My morning walk brings enjoyment and now I am
settled down on the couch to do the dreamwork on last
night's dream. Break time is over.

The first segment:

> ADRIAN AND I ARE MOVING TO A DIFFERENT
> HOME. I CAN SEE THAT MUCH OF OUR STUFF
> IS ALREADY GONE. THERE IS A THREADBARE
> BROWN COUCH. I KNOW WE WILL GET RID OF IT
> AND GET A NEW ONE.

The masculine and feminine are seen in sync, getting
rid of STUFF (issues and memories) and I feel myself
opening up, ready to embrace the "new."

The next segment:

> LATER, I SEE DIMLY THAT ADRIAN IS TRYING
> TO PASS GARBAGE TRUCKS IN THE NIGHT ON
> OUR RIGHT. HE MAKES IT PAST TWO. I SEE
> THAT THERE WAS YET A THIRD, AND I TELL HIM
> SO HE WON'T RUN INTO IT.

As unneeded garbage (*emotional* garbage) is hauled away in the trucks, I want to "get past" it. I have progressed, but the remaining STUFF, the THREAD-BARE COUCH, and not getting past the THIRD truck hint that there may still be work to do. I'm not sure why the feminine is concerned that the masculine might run into the truck . . . is it a signal that it is time for feminine wisdom to take the lead?

The third segment:

> I LOOK IN A MIRROR AND SEE A BRIGHT
> TURQUOISE BAND OF COLOR AROUND MY
> HAIR ON BOTH SIDES FROM EAR TO EAR,
> MADE WITH EVEN, PERFECT LINES LIKE IT WAS
> CAREFULLY APPLIED.

Word association: BAND, combo, small music group . . . Pastor Henry has been talking about wanting to get a contemporary service started at church, complete with a praise band. Is this dream suggesting that I should offer to play in the band? When the BAND is drawn on paper, it looks Egyptian or Native American. The color, TURQUOISE, is a Native American color . . . is the Native American theme emerging again?

There is one more segment:

> *I LATER COME TO A BUILDING AND GO INTO A ROOM THAT HAS WILD CATS. I SIT DOWN ON THE EDGE OF SOME STEPS AND WATCH THEM WALK AROUND THE BIG ROOM. I NOTICE A VERY SMALL COUGAR KITTEN/CUB, NO BIGGER THAN MY HAND. I PICK IT UP AND GENTLY PET IT. I THINK THE MOTHER WILL SURELY COME AFTER ME FOR HANDLING THIS BABY. BUT . . . NO MOTHER COMES.*

Here I am again! It doesn't matter whether it is outer life or inner—I am being presented with wild babies. Just as I wrote about in my piece for the writers' workshop this week, I am forever trying to save abandoned animal babies, no matter how unsuccessful my attempts are! Even though experience and wisdom have taught me that I can't replace an animal baby's parent, my heart *always* moves me to try again. In the dream, my heart says "Yes" to the little COUGAR. Am I not learning from Wisdom? Or are matters of the heart and soul a stronger pull than practical knowledge in determining my behavior and choices?

When I first met the COUGAR in a dream fourteen years ago, it was while recording dreams and working on my inner awareness through non-Christian meditation and workshops, but not attending church or reading Scripture. It was through embracing this symbol of feminine power and tapping her fierce strength that I was able to separate from Tim and follow through with and heal from the divorce.

I thought that when I came back to my Christian faith, I was done with her! I even gave away that Carl

Brender cougar print because it represented a sort of idol (although I had never prayed to the cat!). Yet, three years later, the COUGAR is back in my dreams. It appears I have come full circle. Only this time I see the furry COUGAR CUB as a dream symbol—not an insult to the Creator God at all, but one of the Divine's symbols for instruction and growth.

The COUGAR represents feminine power, but, in my past dreams of the COUGAR, she was always an adult. Why is this one depicted as a BABY? Is there no MOTHER cougar? Am I to adopt this BABY—to keep—once and for all? Or, is she adopting me? Hmmm . . .

Intuitively I feel certain that this little dream segment marks a turning point in my dream crash course, but I am not sure why. Maybe the end of these lessons is in sight! By re-embracing the feminine and the wisdom available through her, I feel ready to embrace wherever these weeks of dreaming are leading me. If I *am* supposed to set a new course in my outer life, I wish I could glimpse a hint of what it might be.

ঔৎড়ঔ

**March 19, 2007**

Since my "rainbow walk," the FLYING SHIP dream, and through these weeks of intense dreamwork, I have been patiently working and waiting for direction, for the Holy Spirit to give me a sign of what God wants me to do.

Last night, as Adrian lay beside me in bed, I heard him speak in his sleep. But, this time he wasn't arguing with his usual dream bad guys; his voice was gentle and calm as he uttered, "I wish I knew how many times I had to teach it—journalism." Hmmm . . . More than once in the last few days, Adrian has prodded, "Why don't you write a book?" I quickly dismissed the notion each time, but are his sleeping words about "journalism" some sort of sign? Should I take them seriously?

∂∞∾

The dream I remember from last night had five segments. In the first segment:

> *I AM AT A LOVELY RESORT. WHEN I LOOK OUT BACK I SEE TWO FLOWERING BUSHES AND THINK THAT MOM WOULD LIKE THIS PLACE. I HELP FOR A WHILE IN THE KITCHEN. THEY HAVE SOME VERY UNUSUAL DISHES, LIKE "ONIONS IN OIL." THE FOOD IS EXCELLENT. BUT THE KITCHEN IS VERY HOT, AND THE STAFF GETS REALLY HOT.*

As I woke up, I immediately recognized that the RESORT is Mohican State Park where Adrian and I visited last fall. I also dreamed about this park a few weeks ago, at the beginning of this dream course! That dream showed me what was causing my neck and shoulder pain and what was leading to my headaches. It was because of that dream that I started going to the chiropractor and started feeling *so* much better. Last night I had a sore throat before going to bed and felt as if I was coming down with something. While thinking about the dream this morning, I focused on the sautéed ONIONS IN OIL and thought about how food symbols in my dreams usually point to a health issue. So, I decided to try some sautéed ONIONS IN OIL this afternoon . . . and my sore throat has disappeared! This is the second time this Native-American-themed park has been the symbolic location of healing for me!

What does it mean that this time I am not just a visitor at this RESORT; I am at work in a very HOT, busy KITCHEN, creating and cooking up dishes, providing nourishment for the diners? Does it represent my progress with this dreamwork to have moved up from being a visitor to being an employee, a worker, learning from the chefs in the KITCHEN where the HOT (vital) work is being done?

The symbolism of the twin images of the FLOWERING BUSHES isn't clear yet, but mentioning THAT MOM WOULD LIKE THIS PLACE draws me back to the original impetus for this dreamwork—her statement, "IT'S A MATTER OF FAITH." Am I close to learning more about what she meant?

୧୨

In the second dream segment:

> I AM IN A BALCONY, AS IN A CHURCH, WHERE
> MUSICIANS HAVE THEIR EQUIPMENT. THEY
> SEEM TO BE PART OF AN ORCHESTRA OR
> MARCHING BAND. THE BAND DIRECTOR
> ASKS ME TO CLEAN UP THE CLOTHES STREWN
> AROUND. I TRY TO DO THIS BUT DON'T WANT TO
> GET THE BAND MEMBERS' CLOTHES MIXED UP,
> SO I PUT THEIR CLOTHES IN THEIR INDIVIDUAL
> BAGS. I AM TEMPTED TO CLEAN UP MORE, LIKE
> THE KNICK-KNACKS ON A SHELF, BUT I DON'T
> KNOW WHICH BELONG TO THE BAND DIRECTOR
> AND WHICH ARE SIMPLY DECORATIONS THAT
> BELONG ON THE BALCONY. I WALK THROUGH

*AISLES OF PEWS; SOME OF THE MUSICIANS ARE
NOT THERE. MAYBE THEY ARE OFF PERFORMING.
ALL OF THE BAND MEMBERS' SHIRTS ARE PINK.*

I am stumped. I need to review the rest of the dream scenes to be able to decipher this segment's meaning and its unfamiliar symbols. Is the BAND DIRECTOR similar to the symbol of the EDUCATIONAL ADMINISTRATOR? What is he trying to tell me? Maybe if I simply follow the circular structure of the dream, this part might become clear later.

In the third segment, I am back at Mohican State Park:

*I AM IN THE MOTEL ROOM. I AM BY MYSELF
STARTING TO CLEAN UP. I HEAR NOISES OUTSIDE
. . . TALKING. I OPEN MY DOOR AND WALK TO THE
WINDOW ACROSS THE HALLWAY. I LOOK OUT
AND SEE A PRETTY WOMAN WITH LONG, BLOND
HAIR AND HER BOYFRIEND DUMPING GARBAGE
INTO THE LOWER DRIVEWAY. THEY ACT AS IF
WHAT THEY ARE DOING IS HELPFUL FOR THE
MOTEL, BUT IT IS A MESS! I LOOK FOR THE KEY
TO CALL THE FRONT DESK TO LET THEM KNOW,
SO THEY CAN QUESTION THE COUPLE. WHEN I
WAS PACKING UP, I COULD SEE DOWN THE HALL
THAT OTHERS WERE COMING TO MOVE IN. I
SAY, "I'M STILL IN THESE ROOMS!" A WOMAN
SAYS, "OH! SORRY!" I ASK THE MAID WHAT
TIME CHECKOUT IS. SHE SAYS 2 P.M., WHICH IS
IN TEN MINUTES, SO I HURRY. THEN I SEE THE
SAME BLOND WOMAN IN THE HALL SMILING AT
ME! I PULL THE MAID ASIDE TO TELL HER THAT
THIS IS THE WOMAN WHO PUT THE TRASH IN
THE DRIVEWAY BELOW THE ROOM!*

This dream concerns me both at the inner and the outer levels. I don't understand why all the GARBAGE is being dumped below my MOTEL ROOM. I am aware in the dream that I've spent night after night having dreams about getting rid of unwanted garbage. Why is it all being brought back?! Why does my dreamself LOOK FOR THE KEY TO CALL THE FRONT DESK? Why not a telephone? Is the word, "KEY," some kind of clue? Arrrgh! I am as frustrated with this segment as with the one before. What are the dream characters doing?! I'm going on to the fourth segment:

> *I AM WITH ADRIAN IN A CAR READY TO LEAVE THE MOTEL, BUT WE ARE HEADING LEFT, WHICH, I SOMEHOW KNOW, IS THE WRONG WAY. WE TURN AROUND AND REALIZE WE ARE STANDING IN A CREEK. ALL WAYS BACK TO OUR CAR ARE BLOCKED. WE HAVE TO GET OUT AND WALK INTO THE LODGE'S BACK ENTRANCE, INTO THE HOT KITCHEN. ADRIAN GOES INTO THE KITCHEN FIRST AND HAS TO CLIMB THROUGH AN OVEN TO GET FROM THE KITCHEN TO THE DINING ROOM! I FOLLOW HIM AND CRAWL THROUGH MYSELF. I MAKE IT OKAY AND WALK AROUND THE TABLES OF DINERS TO GET TO THE LOBBY IN ORDER TO LEAVE.*

The idea that LEFT (the direction to the inner dreamworld) is the WRONG WAY, marks a significant change. And, because we are no longer in our CAR (the dream journey vehicle) and are prevented from getting back into it, I sense again that my crash course in dreamwork is almost finished. But still, I just don't get where this is going.

This fourth dream segment brings me full circle back to the first segment because, again, the FLOWERING BUSHES and the same comment repeats in my mind:

> "MOM WOULD LIKE THIS PLACE." THIS TIME I SEE THE COUPLE DOWN BELOW DUMPING MORE GARBAGE AND THEN FALLING BACK IN IT, HAPPY AT WHAT THEY ARE DOING. I WONDER IF THEY WILL PUT DIRT OVER IT AND USE IT AS A LANDFILL.

Why would MOM LIKE THIS PLACE? What do the FLOWERING BUSHES represent? Why is this crazy COUPLE FALLING happily BACK in the GARBAGE below the MOTEL/ LODGE? And, why do I have to LEAVE? Is my dreamwork course really over?

I am in awe of the fifth and final segment—this little dream finale:

> I AM WITH SOMEONE. I AM SITTING ON HIS LEFT. HE IS ON MY RIGHT (OUTER). I KNOW HE IS A VERY IMPORTANT AUTHORITY, WHO HAS A BOOK OPEN. I KNOW HE REVEALS DREAM MEANINGS WHEN I GET STUCK. I ASK A FEW QUESTIONS. THEN HE SAYS, "WELL, ARE YOU READY TO WRITE THE BOOK?" I REACT WITH SURPRISE AND FEAR. "NO! I DON'T KNOW ENOUGH. THEY WILL ASK ME QUESTIONS I CAN'T ANSWER!"

Whoa! I had forgotten this part. Now I remember how I awakened with a deep sense of reverence—it felt like an encounter with someone higher up! The only part of this entity that I saw was his bare upper arm and the BOOK he was holding on his lap. Is it the BOOK I am supposed to write?

As I think about this last segment, the meanings of the first four perplexing segments start to unfold. And, most importantly, the connection between symbols from past dreams, especially ones from the last ten days, fall into place.

### The Symbols

1) the dream helper who gave me directions for organizing all of my dreamwork and developing a *table of contents*

2) the PREGNANT LADY in the BACK of the GARBAGE TRUCK; (give birth to *what?*)

3) the SEMI-TRUCK in COLORADO being prepared to be placed into my POCKET; (I'm just *lubricating* it!)

4) the blank spiritual quadrant; (I can't dance until I *do something*)

5) the ADMINISTRATOR/NUN who tells me about what can and cannot be taught; and (but I'm a social worker, not an *educator*)

6) Adrian prodding me to write a *book*, and then his dream-word—*"journalism"*

Chills! I am seeing that these connections are finally telling me what this crash course has been leading to! It is sinking in that this dreamwork isn't just for my *own* growth. It makes sense, especially if the information will help other dream travelers! The contents of the dreams, the interpretations of the symbols, and the issues will be personal and unique to me, but the general dream lessons learned may be common and helpful to other beginning dreamers.

The dream helper once again leaves the dream hanging with a question and doesn't respond to my protest. I am embarrassed at my dreamself's whiny reaction. While I wouldn't be the first person to express self-doubt in response to a request from the Divine, I have come to respect the Spirit-guided wisdom of the dreams to such an extent that I am ashamed of my lack of trust. I have to remind myself that Spirit has been patient with me, and remember that throughout the Bible God shows His steadfast patience with those who are slow to catch on and embrace what is being offered.

૨૦૯

After reviewing and taking in the fifth segment, I can interpret the rest of the dream. I am awed and excited!

The church BALCONY represents where the dreaming and dreamwork occur—a higher, spiritual place of learning. The ORCHESTRA represents a collection of dream stories that work together as a whole. In outer life, a MARCHING BAND moves in sync. The music it plays has various themes and instrumental parts, and blends to produce an integrated performance. An ORCHESTRA tells stories through its music and teaches the listener something about life itself.

In asking me to CLEAN UP THE CLOTHES, the BAND DIRECTOR is really telling me to organize the material that needs to be compiled. The sentence, "I DON'T WANT TO

GET THE BAND MEMBERS' CLOTHES MIXED UP," means that I must keep the symbols and their particular dream lessons together. So, their CLOTHES (the dream material) are placed in INDIVIDUAL BAGS (chapters). I AM TEMPTED TO CLEAN UP MORE (incorporate additional outside material), but decide to stick with what the band director has told me. I WALK THROUGH AISLES OR PEWS; SOME OF THE MUSICIANS AREN'T THERE, MAYBE THEY ARE OFF PERFORMING. This tells me that, as I review the past dreamwork material, it is okay to leave out certain dreams, especially very personal or revealing dreams that cover confidential issues. THE BAND MEMBERS' SHIRTS WERE ALL PINK. All the information I have is in sync, just as the masculine and feminine are now in sync. PINK is the color of love—this is a project of love given by the Divine, the source of all love and dreams.

The third segment, which takes place in the MOTEL ROOM, tells me that this particular dreamwork course is a temporary place from which I will be moving on. It now has to be cleaned up. The copious paperwork has to be put in order. In the dream, when I LOOK OUTSIDE MY ROOM to see who is TALKING, I see that the masculine and feminine, who are working together, are bringing all of the GARBAGE back and placing it below the MOTEL ROOM— below the place where I have been doing the dreaming and dreamwork. But in the dream I don't get what they are doing, because I don't yet know that I am to use this GARBAGE—these memories and stories—to write a BOOK! If I had been paying attention, I might have seen that the word "KEY" tells me that this GARBAGE scene is *key* to understanding the dream.

The COUPLE is DUMPING MORE GARBAGE and FALLING happily BACK in it. The fate of the couple from the GARBAGE TRUCK dream is finally revealed! Now I understand that the PREGNANT LADY in the back of the GARBAGE TRUCK was nurturing the inner knowledge *and* the book I am supposed to "give birth to"! They bring the GARBAGE *back* because I now have to revisit it to write about this journey. Perhaps the THIRD TRUCK of my earlier dream contained this garbage and we followed it!

When I think of this *mountain* of garbage, I think of how a mountain—a scenic landscape—can be created from discarded "stuff." I looked up the word LANDFILL in the dictionary: "A method of rehabilitating land in which garbage and trash are buried in low lying ground to build it up." How perfect an image is this? Getting rid of the garbage would have been wrong thinking. I *need* to remember these life experiences, dreams, and feelings, because by understanding them, I will learn to become the person I am meant to be—with them, Divine Wisdom is building a beautiful mountain!

ॐ

As the dream continues, I remain irritated and suspicious. In truth, I don't think I am ready to stop this dream course. But I am told that CHECKOUT time is very soon—*10 MINUTES*. When I looked up the number ten as a symbol this morning, I was reminded that it is the number of completeness, of a circle closing in on itself! Have I come full circle?

In the fourth segment, when the masculine and I TURN AROUND and head RIGHT (outer), I now understand that it means it is no longer time for me to journey, but to *journal*. It's time to do the spiritual (CREEK) work on foot—to make sense of this thrilling experience and share it. We proceed into the HOT KITCHEN from the first segment—this is the dream's symbol for the writing of the book! It certainly sounds like there is a lot of HOT, hard work to be done.

When the masculine and I finish in the KITCHEN, we CRAWL through the OVEN, a place where something (a manuscript?) can be cooked, baked, or completed. I walk around the TABLE OF DINERS. They may be other beginning dream-travelers working at their own tables (where life's learning takes place), and, perhaps benefitting from a similar dream-course, or maybe even eating and digesting the meal (book?) I worked on in the KITCHEN.

We finally get to the lobby and I look out at the TWO FLOWERING BUSHES. I can now see that *they* are the end result—the blossoms or fruit of this dreamwork. I know that my mother, who started this journey with her statement, "IT'S A MATTER OF FAITH," WOULD LIKE THIS PLACE. And I can't help feeling she would be happy with what her words put in motion!

৵৹ঔ

After finishing the dreamwork today, I looked again at the dream from yesterday morning. In the dream, *I KNOW WE WILL GET RID OF THE THREADBARE BROWN COUCH AND GET A NEW ONE*. Of course! The couch is the place where my dreamwork is done in outer life. It has been well used, but now it is time to GET A NEW ONE and tackle this *new* project ahead of me.

In last night's dream, the BLOND WOMAN IS SMILING at me because she knows that all along I have wanted the garbage truck to take my garbage, baggage, sins, etc., away—and I thought that was, indeed, what has been happening. But she has brought it all back and dumped it beneath the very building where I am to write. It is to be used for fodder, for building up the land, for compost for the FLOWERING BUSHES, for the stories that dreams use to help heal.

Now I realize the twin purposes for all of this dreamwork: my own healing and renewal, and to share this story with others. Are these the TWO FLOWERING BUSHES? Maybe I am being asked to write down these lessons so that people interested in doing dreamwork can see better how to do it from the outset. Maybe it will help show them, as I was shown, how to embrace their own humanness, and develop a closer connection to God by learning how to have a conversation with their soul.

I can't believe it! As I am writing this, I hear the garbage truck outside the living room window.

*Lessons I am Learning about Dreamwork*

Lesson #27

**Symbol and Metaphor Deciphering.** Dream language is, for the most part, a metaphorical language through which an issue in inner and/or outer life is presented. To decipher the dream's message, I need to understand the "language," which means I need to think about what the story and its symbols represent for me. In the dream story of the MOUNTAIN OF GARBAGE, I realize a two-fold message: with respect to my outer, physical world, I am supposed to revisit the emotional GARBAGE to help share my experience of healing with others; with respect to my inner, subconscious world, I am not meant to get rid of the GARBAGE as I had thought—it is a foundation for my inner growth and healing.

*One of the most important things we need to learn is to be open to this spiritual world because here we can recognize God's hand even more clearly than in the physical world that surrounds us.*

**Morton Kelsey**[1]

*And without faith it is impossible to please God, because anyone who comes to him must believe that he exists and that he rewards those who earnestly seek him.*

**Hebrews 11:6**[2]

*Courage is itself a source of joy and we can seek it from the wild, the untamed God, who runs such risks for me. We need courage so that we can dare to leave the land of slavery and walk boldly and joyfully through the dangerous waters and the barren deserts. Only there can we learn to sing and laugh, for wherever we let God lead us will be our promised land.*

**Sara Maitland**[3]

Chapter 18

## *Learning What's "Key"*

Dream: *Hardheaded Herbert*

**March 21, 2007**

Well, I now know I am to write a book, but this morning's dream confuses me because it seems to go back to dealing with old memories and baggage. Why didn't it come earlier—prior to the MOHICAN MARCHING ORDERS dream and my revelation of writing a book? I thought the dream course was wrapping up—winding down . . .

The first segment:

I AM TRAVELING WITH ADRIAN AND SOME FRIENDS. WE ARRIVE AT A PLACE THAT HOLDS A PAINFUL MEMORY FOR ME FROM 40 YEARS AGO. I AM SUPPOSED TO HAVE A MEETING WITH HERB. WE HAVE NOT BEEN A COUPLE IN A LONG TIME, BUT WE WERE ONCE SO CLOSE. I GO TO SEE HIM AT HIS OFFICE. HE IS NOT THERE SO I GIVE HIS SECRETARY THE MANUSCRIPT THAT I WROTE. I RESPECT HIM AND APPARENTLY WANT HIM TO SEE THIS MANUSCRIPT.

Is the MANUSCRIPT the book that needs to be written? The dream continues:

*I AM ACCOMPANIED BY THREE GIRLFRIENDS TO A BEAUTIFUL GREEN PARK WHERE I AM TO MEET HIM. I FINALLY SEE HIM COMING—OLDER, THINNER, AND SUNBURNED . . . AND NOT AT ALL HAPPY TO SEE ME! THIS IS A SIGNIFICANT CONTRAST TO THE BEAUTIFUL GREEN SETTING.*

*HE SITS DOWN AND WANTS TO KNOW WHY I HAVE COME, BUT THEN HE RAMBLES ON ABOUT OTHER THINGS. I ASK ABOUT HIS BEING SUNBURNED. HE SAYS THAT HE AND HIS WIFE WERE OUTSIDE THE WHOLE DAY BEFORE. I WAS HOPING THERE WOULD BE SOME RECOGNITION AND TENDERNESS IN HIM BECAUSE OF OUR PAST TOGETHER; BUT EITHER HE DOESN'T CARE AND HAS PUT IT BEHIND HIM, OR HE HAS FORGOTTEN BECAUSE OF HIS OLD AGE. I STAND IN FRONT OF HIM. I NEVER SIT DOWN. HE GETS UP AND IS STILL RAMBLING AS HE WALKS OFF DOWN THE STREET. I HALF WONDER IF HE WILL BE BACK, BUT I KNOW HE PROBABLY WILL NOT RETURN.*

I am so saddened by his walking away and his lack of recognition! The same grief was felt when our relationship ended. My dreamself wants the same thing now that I wanted then—recognition, attention, and caring. But it is clear that, once again, the relationship is not meant to be.

The second segment continues:

*I AM STANDING WITH MY GIRLFRIENDS TRYING TO DECIDE WHAT TO DO NEXT. I FEEL EMPTY AND JUST WANT TO GO SOMEWHERE AND CRY—*

*ALTHOUGH THE GIRLFRIENDS ARE TALKING ABOUT LUNCH, AS IT IS ALMOST NOON. I TELL THEM TO GO AHEAD, THAT I WILL JOIN THEM LATER. THEN I PROCEED TO WALK THE WOODSY PATH BACK TO THE HOTEL WHERE WE ARE ALL STAYING. ONE OF MY FRIENDS FOLLOWS BEHIND ME. I CAN TELL SHE DOESN'T WANT TO LEAVE ME ALONE. SHE WANTS ME TO TALK ABOUT HOW I FEEL. I SAY, "THERE IS A TIME FOR GIRLFRIENDS TO HELP, BUT RIGHT NOW I JUST WANT TO BE ALONE AND CRY." SHE DISAGREES AND WILL NOT LEAVE ME.*

*ON THE WOODSY PATH, I FIND AND PICK UP AN EMPTY, DECORATIVE GLASS, LIKE AN OLD JELLY GLASS. IT IS LIKE THE ONES FROM THE 1950s THAT JELLY OR PEANUT BUTTER CAME IN. IT HAS A COLORFUL DESIGN—A REDDISH COLOR. WHEN I PICK IT UP, IT HAS A BLACKISH LEAF OR PIECE OF DIRT FROM THE TRAIL HANGING ON THE BOTTOM OF IT. I THINK ABOUT TAKING IT BACK TO THE HOTEL, BUT I SET IT BACK DOWN ON THE GROUND. THE GIRLFRIEND, WHO IS WALKING BEHIND ME PICKS UP THE GLASS, BRINGS IT WITH US, AND TURNS IT IN TO THE HOTEL PEOPLE. I REALIZE THAT I SHOULD HAVE DONE THAT.*

A WOODSY PATH, a place I like to WALK in outer life, reminds me of how I often take solace in nature and outdoors, but never turn to *people* when help is needed to make sense of things. The dream FRIEND wants me to talk about HOW I FEEL—something I am not comfortable with. Growing up, I was never asked how I *felt*, at least not about serious things like Dad's drinking or Margaret hiding in my closet—I was taught to go to my room until I calmed down. When I say, *"THERE IS A TIME FOR GIRLFRIENDS TO HELP,"* but *not now*, the helper *WILL NOT LEAVE ME.* She is modeling the caring adult that I needed as a child!

The *DECORATIVE JELLY GLASS* is similar to the ones Mom used to wash out and keep in the cupboard to use as drinking glasses . . . I see it as symbol of a time gone by, such as my relationship with *HERB.* The *GLASS* once held sweet *JELLY,* but now it is *EMPTY;* the relationship is gone. The *BLACKISH PIECE OF DIRT* hanging from the bottom of it is a kind of reminder that, at some level, the pain of ending the relationship still lingers. I *SET THE GLASS BACK DOWN,* rejected. My dreamself wants to leave the *GLASS* behind . . . just like when I wanted to leave all my garbage and pain behind. But, the helper friend *PICKS IT UP* and *BRINGS IT WITH US*—back into my life like the *GARBAGE* the *COUPLE* brought back to the motel in my dream two days ago.

In the third segment, Adrian and I are outside the door to our room at the hotel:

> *ADRIAN HAS LOST HIS KEY. I PULL MINE OUT*
> *AND WE ENTER THE ROOM.*

Here is that word "*KEY*" again! I know now that when the image or word "*KEY*" appears in a dream, it is a tipoff that the next segment will be significant, or "*KEY,*" to understanding the whole dream.

> *ADRIAN CARRIES IN OUR CLOTHES. THIS*
> *CONFUSES ME. WE CAME TO THIS HOTEL WITH*
> *THREE OTHER COUPLES, BUT I THOUGHT THAT*
> *THE FOUR MEN WERE STAYING TOGETHER IN*
> *THEIR ROOM AND WE FOUR WOMEN IN OURS.*

I am falling back to my old ways of trying to keep the masculine and feminine separated, and as a result, out of sync. In the WOODSY PATH scene, I try to separate from my emotional (feminine) feeling side and suppress how I felt after meeting with HERB. It's as if I'm that child again, trying to go to my ROOM to be alone and calm down.

> MY OLD BLUE TRAIN CASE NEAR THE DOOR. I NOW HAVE A BABY WITH ME—LIKE BABY ELLA—AND I DON'T HAVE HER MILK/FORMULA. IT IS TIME FOR HER TO EAT. I THINK I WILL CALL DOWN TO THE DESK TO SEE IF THEY HAVE POWDERED MILK, BUT I KNOW IT ISN'T THE SAME AS FORMULA.
>
> I THINK ABOUT HOW TO FIX A BABY BOTTLE— THREE LEVEL SCOOPS PER SIX OUNCES. I REALIZE THAT I HAVEN'T BEEN PUTTING IN THE FULL AMOUNT OF FORMULA THAT IS NEEDED, WHICH CAUSES HER BOTTLES TO BE WATERY. NOW I KNOW WHAT TO DO, THE CORRECT WAY TO MAKE IT. I HOLD HER CLOSE ON MY SHOULDER.

Originally I used that OLD BLUE TRAIN CASE in the late 50s and early 60s, and as recently as a few years ago. Does it signify that the dream deals with an issue from my past? The color BLUE represents hope—the hope that I might learn what I didn't learn as a child.

The "key" to the symbolic meaning of the OLD BLUE TRAIN CASE is in the word TRAIN. I remember how the dream of the TRAIN falling over, and the separation of the SOUND of the crash, was the image that eventually led me to understand how I separate my feelings from difficult emotional situations. I just remembered something else:

the actual train case had a large mirror on the inside of the lid. When opened, I could see myself. Now, with the dream's help, when I imagine opening it, I can see the emotional "stuff" that got locked inside, and which takes a "KEY," like this dream from the unconscious, to let it out.

The correct FORMULA is needed for a child to be nourished and to grow. In this dream segment, the FORMULA has been watered down, deprived of nourishment. My childhood was watered down in the same way. It was missing the help, explanations, and conversations needed in order for me to grow. But, in these dreams, I am learning the CORRECT WAY TO MAKE IT, to process the things that happen to me, to ask for help and to allow myself to be nourished.

After working with this last segment, I'm not sure that I *am* relapsing into my old ways—instead, it appears that the work I have to do to heal *must* be done by the feminine nourisher.

☙◦⚬

Another realization: I wanted *HERB* to give me some explanation of what our relationship had been about. But, it is up to *me* to figure that out. After doing the dreamwork and meditating on the dream, I now see that what I wanted from him was the affection and attention that I rarely received from Dad. Looking back, I realize that any fatherly attention he had given me stopped at about age ten. Because of that, on some level, I decided that I was not "somebody." My worth was based on the way he interacted and communicated with me. Although he might have truly loved me, his drinking prevented him from being a loving parent. I didn't realize it then, but I sought in my relationships with boyfriends what was lacking in my relationship with him. How sad were the results! It boosted my self-worth every time I won the affection of men, but I didn't understand how to have a healthy relationship. Inevitably, my choice in men were distant like he was.

When I look for a reflection of me in the BOYFRIEND symbol, he represents the "me" who gets crabby and doesn't want to be put on the spot, doesn't want an interruption of life, and doesn't like messes, especially emotionally charged messes. I don't want to revisit an old relationship that didn't work. My preference is to be left alone. He personifies the pain and anger, the rambling irritability, the part of me that doesn't want to deal with issues. That's why he WASN'T THERE at his office where we were supposed to meet; why I had to WAIT for him in the park; why he sat and RAMBLED ON as I stayed standing. This was a defense to put me off so he would not have to talk about this relationship and the impact it had on me. And then, my classic move: walking away.

✑✖

This dramatic dream story and the resulting dreamwork showed me how to look at an old grief in a new way and it enabled me to identify a troubling component of my personality. First I found "Slick Willy," now I have found "Hard-Headed Herbert," the cranky, selfish, hermit aspect of myself revealed in the *HERB* dream character. Now I have a humorous take on a painful and sad memory!

I still don't know why this particular dream comes *after* what appeared to be the winding down of the dream lessons. Maybe it has to do with the critical message of this dream, which is the need to ask for help and confide in friends, or my pastor, or family, in times of difficulty—now and in the years to come. Equally important is knowing that I need to be that listener for others, especially for children.

And, I realize now that it isn't just the heavy emotional stuff I try to deal with on my own; it's even simple, ordinary, everyday issues—a point that was punctuated just a while ago when the computer started to type in a funny backwards way while I was writing. It was stuck and I had no clue what I had done, or how to fix it. So, I was "forced" to call Kathy, and with her help, we got it fixed. Ah, Spirit! You are full of tricky ways to get the point across!

*Lessons I am Learning about Dreamwork:*

**Lesson # 28**

**Insight.** Dream characters all have a gift to give. They reflect a part of myself that I need to recognize and bring to light. Those dream characters to which I have the strongest reaction have the most to reveal about my personality and how I look at life. If they are not especially likeable characters, exploring them will take away their power. Their origins, existence, and the function they serve may be revealed along with a new way for me to respond.

*The dream-spirits are not distant or abstract entities;
they are experienced in visions as living beings that
appear to assist and aid the dreamer
in his everyday encounters.*
**Lee Irwin[1]**

*. . . for you have been my help and in the shadow of
your wings I sing for joy.*
**Psalm 63:7[2]**

*Seek the Lord while he may be found,
call upon him while he is near.*
**Isaiah 55:6[3]**

*If God were to stop speaking the whole created universe
would cease to exist.*
**J. Philip Newell[4]**

Chapter 19

# An Ending and a Beginning

Dreams: *The Jedi Spaceship;*
*A Canadian Park/Ancient Ruins; The Dance*

## March 25, 2007

This morning another dream came to encourage me to explore other religions. This one suggests I learn more about the Abrahamic religions Judaism and Islam — sister religions to Christianity. When I answered the dreamwork question, "what does this dream want me to learn," there were four key points: 1) to not be afraid of spiritual exploration; 2) to explore Jewish and Muslim writers; 3) to learn about the wisdom of ancient religions; and 4) to increase my knowledge of, and experimentation with dreams and the dreamwork process, honoring it as a valid spiritual path that can enhance traditional religious practices.

This dream joins the others that led me to explore about Native American spirituality and symbolism, Christianity's Sophia path of Wisdom, the Divine Feminine face of God, and Celtic spirituality. It seems as if I am being urged to further expand my small, confining perception of God and the Christian experience.

☙❧

## March 27, 2007

It's been nine days since the dream in which I am asked about writing a book. Since then, I have been recording and working with my dreams, carefully watching for a dream or symbol that will tell me when this crash course is actually over and the writing should begin.

My dream last night seems to signal that my initiation course in dreamwork really has finally come to an end! I woke up at midnight able to remember only this segment:

> A RAISED CIRCULAR PLATFORM IS IN THE CENTER OF A LARGER DREAM CIRCLE WITH A REPLICA OF A JEDI SPACESHIP NAMED THE DAMERESTING ON TOP OF THE PLATFORM.

The RAISED PLATFORM image reminds me of the LANDFILL/MOUNTAIN image created by the young couple dumping garbage at the motel. As for the LARGER DREAM CIRCLE, it looks like a circle with dreams on the circumference surrounding the center. It is a reconstruction of the curved comb/ladder image I was given at the beginning of this course in dreamwork—the one that was vertical at first until the helper told me to bend it into a curve so that the ends would be joined! My first interpretation when doing the dreamwork on this dream was that this mandala-shaped image might represent circular dreams: the circle is the whole dream; the individual dream scenes are around the circumference. When I looked at it again, I thought it actually might represent life itself: the circle is life at a higher state of consciousness and understanding; all dreams and life experiences are around the circumference. Maybe this is one way of looking at wholeness.

The next image, A JEDI SPACESHIP, brings back vivid images of the *Star Wars* movie, but the word REPLICA tells me that I am aware that this image is symbolic. During the dreamwork, it brought to mind of the curious literary piece about the FLYING SHIP—the one I just couldn't figure out—that began this dreamwork journey. Now, I wonder why, at what feels like the end of the journey, I am shown another flying ship—a sophisticated SPACESHIP . . .

∽∾

The next dream has three scenes:

> I AM WORKING AT A DESK NEAR MARY. SHE
> GETS UP TO GO OUT. I GET UP TO GO, TOO, AND
> FOLLOW HER OUT. SHE HEARS MY FOOTSTEPS
> AND TURNS SLIGHTLY. I SAY, "I'M FOLLOWING
> YOU!" WE WALK TOGETHER.

This is the call to start writing the book! MARY is my "literary" friend and apparently a symbol for the writer in me. I follow her to join forces with that creative, literary side of myself. This is the signal that I have been waiting for—WE WALK TOGETHER—it's time to start the work!

In the second segment:

> I AM DRIVING IN CANADA. THERE IS A PARK
> ON MY RIGHT. THE OFFICER SAYS HE HAS LIKED
> THE PARK SINCE HE WAS A CHILD BECAUSE IT
> HAS A LOT OF WILDLIFE—ESPECIALLY BIRDS

THAT VISIT. I DECIDE TO GO SEE THIS PARK. AS
I DRIVE INTO THE WOODSY AREA, I SEE A HUGE
BUILDING LIKE AN OLD SCHOOL BUILDING IN
FRONT OF ME. I EXPECT TO SEE IT FALLING
APART, BUT IT LOOKS IN GOOD SHAPE. IN FACT,
IT IS BEING USED FOR A COMMUNITY CENTER.
I SEE BANNERS AND POSTERS OF UPCOMING
EVENTS IN THE FRONT ENTRYWAY. I SEE A
LADY ON A STAGE IN FRONT OF THE BUILDING
CALLING OUT THE RECIPE FOR HER FRENCH
DRESSING. IT HAS GRAPE JAM IN IT. I WANT TO
GET IT BECAUSE I CAN USE MY HOMEMADE JAM
IN IT, BUT SHE IS TALKING TOO FAST. I LIKE
THIS GROUP OF WOMEN, AND I THINK IT WILL
BE A NICE COMMUNITY TO BE A PART OF.

This feels like a "coming home" kind of place, similar
to the beautiful apartment I dreamed about when I first
retired. The WOODSY setting is so welcoming and full
of the WILDLIFE and BIRDS that I love. But, in this case,
"home" is a COMMUNITY setting, not just *my* home. Since
CANADA is north, it denotes a spiritual place or state of
mind and I wonder if this segment may be referring to
the dreamworld in which I have become so comfortable.

I sense that I have been to this park and seen this
building before—so long ago that I EXPECT TO SEE IT
FALLING APART from neglect. The HUGE BUILDING might
symbolize the part of my life that involves introspection,
becoming whole, and being part of a community. I
neglected it by failing to participate in dreamwork or any
secular or religious community life in a significant way.
Or maybe the OLD SCHOOL BUILDING simply represents a
place of learning—where my course in dreamwork was

completed—and it has now become a COMMUNITY CENTER where my experiences will be shared. The PARK *is* on my right, which suggests that this dream will unfold in my outer world. If I carry through and write a book about this work, I will certainly be putting myself out there into the community!

Through my dreams, I have been healed and enlightened, but now I see that that this dreamwork experience has not been just for my own personal growth. The message in this dream calls me to build relationships and, like a COMMUNITY CENTER, act for the growth of the community.

⌒∽

In the third scene of my dream this morning:

> I AM AT A SEASIDE PLACE THIS TIME. I AM WALKING THROUGH AND UNDER A HUGE OLD DILAPIDATED BUILDING WITH GREEK OR ROMAN COLUMNS. IT IS OLD AND UNUSED BECAUSE IT IS A RELIC FROM THE PAST. I GO ON THROUGH TO FIND THE PEOPLE I CAME WITH, WHO ARE ON THE BEACH. SOMEONE IS WALKING BEHIND ME IN THE DISTANCE. I WONDER IF I SHOULD BE AFRAID.

This place, this SEASIDE area, feels like a distant spiritual country and my senses tell me I have been here before. When I woke up to write it out, my attention was focused on the dream figure following me. In a sleepy, meditative state, he catches up with me. As I did with the big man in the white T-shirt, I listened as he "spoke" to me:

HE IS A MAN IN MODERN-DAY CLOTHES, AND
AS HE APPROACHES I ASK IF HE KNOWS ME.
HE SMILES AND SAYS THAT HE WAITS TO HELP
ME WITH THE MEANINGS OF DREAMS. HE SAYS
THAT IT DOESN'T MATTER WHETHER I AM AT
A FIFTY-YEAR-OLD SCHOOL BUILDING IN A
NORTHERN COUNTRY LIKE CANADA OR ACROSS
THE OCEAN 2000 YEARS AGO—THERE WILL
BE A HELPER WAITING TO ASSIST. I STAND IN
COMPLETE SURPRISE AND AWE AND SAY, "YOU!
YOU'RE THE TOGA MAN!"

I ASK THE TOGA MAN ABOUT THE DREAM
HELPERS. HE SAYS THEY ARE FACILITATORS
THAT HELP US GAIN HIGHER WISDOM AND
KNOWLEDGE. THEY ARE FUNCTIONS OF THE
HOLY SPIRIT AND COME TO US THROUGH
OUR HIGHER SELF; THEY ASSIST IN THE
ACCESS TO AND CORRECT INTERPRETATION
OF A DREAM SYMBOL.

The helpers are as equally important to watch for as are
the symbols, but they seem so much a part of the dream
landscape that they often go unnoticed. They are "just
there" and often have no definite appearance other than
a vague, unseen quality of being male or female. They
seem to be of no particular interest or significance at first,
so as not to detract from the dream. But, I know as I've
progressed through this journey, my ability to spot them
has gotten better! Just like the Toga Man and the Man in
the White T-Shirt, I have been able to ask questions of
them, either in the dream or after I've written it down, and
they have helped clarify issues and symbols.

In the *FLYING SHIP* dream from the beginning of this journey, when I felt so clueless about what was happening, I wrote, "*NOW PEOPLE ARE COMING BACK IN A BIG SHIP FLOATING ACROSS THE SKY. THE MAN IN THE TOGA HAS BEEN LEISURELY GOOFING OFF, BUT SEES THE BIG WOODEN SHIP AND KNOWS HE HAS TO PREPARE AND GET DOWN TO WORK. THEY ARE HERE.*" Now here he is, in modern dress, standing with me under an ancient ruin—a metaphor for the timeless way that God speaks through visions and dreams!

❧◈❧

So in this work, as in a complete dream, I come full circle to the place where I started. The meaning of the beginning dream, THE FLYING SHIP, is now revealed. The typewriter was pushed back between the cabinets and the anchor was upside down in the corner because it was time to fly—to dream the dreams! I was being set loose in my dreamworld—free to sail on this dreamwork excursion. Now, at the end, it is time to pull the typewriter back out!

The picture I sketched in February of the FLYING SHIP is a lovely wooden frigate with its sails billowing out in the wind. It is a ship one expects to find "at home" in water. Water is a symbol both for the spiritual realm and for the unconscious depths. And yet, this ship flies! The Hebrew word for wind, *ruach*, is the same word for breath and spirit. This flying ship full of people is being blown by the breath of God—by the Holy Spirit. It is a metaphor for the many nighttime journeys taken in these last two months, and that I will keep on taking in the future, with the many dream characters and helpers that fill my dream landscapes. My world is different from the world I knew before. This intense spiritual experience has changed me.

I feel like an explorer who is learning to use an ancient, spiritual-communication "force" to explore, navigate, and learn the wondrous mysteries of the Divine, of myself, and of what wholeness and humanness mean. "DAME" is a good name for the JEDI SPACESHIP! It is the vessel for my higher self.

Now, like THE MAN IN THE TOGA, I know it is time to PREPARE and GET DOWN TO WORK—to *write*—so others may learn and embark on their own amazing journeys!

❦

## March 31, 2007

I woke up from this morning's dream full of joy!

> *MY HAIR IS DONE UP IN BLOND CURLS. I AM*
> *HAPPY, JOYFUL, AND DANCING! THE YOUNG*
> *MAN COMES UP AND DANCES WITH ME. I AM*
> *DOING A FAST TAP-DANCE, ALMOST AN INDIAN*
> *DANCE . . . JUST THE TWO OF US.*

What a voyage it has been! The end *is* the beginning and the beginning *is* the end. The journey to wholeness and to embracing humanness—and the Divine Spark within—is a circular path. Some would say a spiral. We are on the journey at any point and it is *all* a journey around the still point—GOD, Great Spirit, Allah, Yahweh—the Nameless One who has inspired, guided, comforted, warned, and taught for thousands of years . . . in dreams and in life. Our part is to pay attention!

# PART VII

# INTEGRATION AND

# ACTION

*The voices people hear in a dream or vision are addressed specifically to them and their situations and lead one to conclude that each individual has already received an outline for his or her life and need only to realize their unique inherent possibilities.*
**Vine Deloria[1]**

*So I say to you, ask, and it will be given you; search and you will find; knock and the door will be opened for you.*
*If you then, who are evil, know how to give good gifts to your children, how much more will the heavenly Father give the Holy Spirit to those who ask him.*
**Luke 11:9 & 13[2]**

*Word from God eternal springing, fill our minds, we pray; And in all artistic vision give integrity; May the flame within us burning kindle yearning day by day.*
**Text: David Mowbray[3]**

*To make the poem of our faith, we must learn not to settle for a false certitude but to embrace ambiguity and mystery.*
**Kathleen Norris[4]**

Chapter 20

## An Ancient Call

**August 1, 2007**

The manuscript is nearly finished and I am amazed that it has fallen into seven segments just like the curved mandala from the dream at the beginning of my journey and the platform in the *JEDI SPACESHIP* dream. I now believe that the pattern of Discernment, Forgiveness, Understanding, Healing, Compassion/Growth, Guidance, and Integration/Action is the process that meaningful dreams follow to help us understand ourselves. It seems to be the very path that leads to wholeness and connectedness to our inner Self and the Divine.

As my dreamwork has been progressing, I have increasingly felt a strong urge to go back to Mariemont and visit the places where I grew up. The village has so often seemed a spiritual home in my dreams; the beautiful apartment I dreamed of in 2004 was there. So, today I went, not in search of anything in particular, simply obeying the inner prompting of my heart. I felt excited and had to fight off the urge to ask a friend along because I understood this was about my past. I had to be quiet to hear any whispers of Spirit.

In the first place I stopped, I found books about the history of Mariemont. I learned that the land I grew up on, where I played, swam, and walked, was also a home and burial ground of the Fort Ancient culture of Native Americans from 1450 to the late 1500s.

The Shawnee resided there until the late 1700s. How did I not know that? Mariemont is known as the "Madisonville Site" and was a major archeological site in the 1800s and is famous in the world of archaeology!

I drove to all five of the houses we lived in, to the bluff that overlooks the Little Miami, and then to the swimming pool. Next to the swimming pool parking lot, there was a park and a shelter house, dedicated in 2001 to the Fort Ancient culture on whose burial ground I was standing. No wonder I felt so at home and at peace at that Fort Ancient powwow in Oregonia I went to a few weeks ago—Native American spirits surrounded me every day of my life for eighteen years! I lived and walked on sacred ground all my life until I left for college!

When I stopped for lunch at a little deli, I sat outside and fed the friendly sparrows, and thought about Mom's statement, *"It's a matter of faith."* Have I found the answer to that rhetorical statement? That depends. Like all dream symbols, Mom's statement doesn't mean just one thing. It is as simple or as complicated as the context within which I am viewing it. If her statement pertains to this wonderful experience of dreams, visions, and dreamwork, I have learned that it takes faith and trust. I have had to place a wholehearted trust in the Holy Spirit's lead and direction in order to follow this intricate and enlightening process.

Her statement might also imply, *"What* do I believe," which is a different matter. I am comfortable in my traditional, liturgical church, and yet I know that the Triune God is much more than what the Creeds disclose. Through this dream journey, this process of growth, I have gotten over those things of the past that have had a hold on me and found that God loves me wholeheartedly. When I felt His grace, something broke open inside of me, letting in new ideas and experiences of Him that I wouldn't have been open to before the dreamwork. My dreams have encouraged me to explore the many religious systems of the earth. By studying their holy wisdom I have come to understand that loving God and having a closer relationship with God is not so much about *what* I believe after all. It is about trusting the Nameless One.

I've come to realize that the times in my life when I felt empty and disconnected from the Divine were my own doing. I had not been able to embrace and learn from my brokenness, nor to actively dedicate my life, my actions, and my thoughts to my Creator.

Maybe it is only by experiencing sin, separation, and the difficult times in life that we can appreciate the great joy of an active and loving relationship with God, when we, as the prodigal son or daughter, return. And when we do, the Nameless One is waiting to embrace us with countless affirmations. By listening to the Ancient Call of synchronistic events and dreams, our eyes are opened to the "Way" of *meaning*, the symbolic language of God's kingdom, which is a pearl of inordinate price.

. . . *to be spiritual, you (your ego) must let the*

*Spirit be the Spirit. For many, to be spiritual is to*

*possess the Spirit, to have the Spirit.*

*As they are with most other things,*

*such folks feel the need to be in control of the Spirit.*

*But once you think you control the Spirit,*

*what you are controlling is not the Spirit.*

*The enlivening Spirit of God within us*

*cannot be controlled.*

*We must give up control and accept our fundamental*

*existential vulnerability.*

*Such vulnerability, which the ego so dislikes, is*

*essential to the life of the spirit.*

*Vulnerability, we should remember, is a function of*

*trust, a core value in the ethos of Jesus.*

*Or as Paul said, 'If we live by the Spirit, let us also be*

*guided by the Spirit' (Galatians 5:25).*

**- C.S. Song**[5]

# Epilogue

## Coming Full Circle

My journey did not end when I finished the manuscript. In fact, I felt a bit lost when the Holy Spirit became eerily quiet about it. The guidance had been so clear during the six weeks of dreamwork and the subsequent writing, but suddenly it was as if Spirit had simply turned off the transmission and I didn't know what to do with the manuscript. *What's going on, Holy Spirit? Was all of this work just for my own learning? Is there something more I am supposed to be doing with this?* When no answer came, all I could do was have faith that in time I would receive one. The manuscript was placed in an empty bottled-water box, where it sat so long in a corner of our enclosed back porch that a couple of spiders made their home in it.

What I didn't realize was that a way forward was being constructed! Like the COMMUNITY CENTER in my dream, I reached out to friends and the women in my writers' group, who encouraged me to send the manuscript to publishers. While searching for a publisher, I encountered Joyce Rockwood Hudson's *Natural Spirituality: Recovering the Wisdom Tradition in Christianity*. Here was someone who was also drawn into dreamwork by the Holy Spirit and then asked to write a book about it! Joyce's experience came twenty years before mine, but I was astounded at the similarity of the images in her book with those in my dreams. It affirmed the validity of the information I had been given in my own dreams and confirmed for me that dream symbols may be universal, or at least similar in a particular culture.

Ultimately I had a lovely meeting with Joyce and acted on her suggestion to rewrite the manuscript as a journal. During that rewriting, three years later, I was able to look at the dreams with new insight. Although I had learned a great deal during those intense weeks of dreaming back in 2007, it wasn't until the rewriting that the threads that ran through those dreams got connected. I couldn't see the weaving in its entirety until time passed, and until I had completed the task of making the work more understandable—something I wasn't able to do when writing the first draft. Originally, I thought each lesson that came to me, each dream, was separate—each distinct from the one before and the one that followed. Even when I could see that some themes were being carried over, I never saw the whole picture. I think this stems from the fact that at that time, when dreamwork was so new to me, I never imagined that our dreams have such continuity and integration. Only now am I able to see the degree to which they all fit together. Although the majority of what I have written I truly understood during the dreamwork process, rewriting it enabled me to reveal to the reader a slightly greater understanding of the dreams than I originally had. It was an amazing journey!

৵৽৹

During the time of working on the rewrite, I often smelled smoke—the smoke of burning sage and occasionally the smoke of a campfire. It wasn't there *only* during the writing—it would happen at various times throughout the day; it was a presence that seemed to be always with me. Over the last few days I have been meditating on the INDIAN HEAD symbol and asking Spirit to help me understand what it was that I was missing when I first encountered it. I was feeling restless—why the Native American theme? Slowly, as my waking brain stepped out of the way, the message started to unfold.

The dream journey actually started three years earlier, in 2004, with the dream of a beautiful apartment, a beloved home. It is this I seek. A home is also what my Native American friends seek—a home of woodsy forests and meadows that they once loved to roam. The natural world speaks to them: the animals, plants, streams, sky, birds . . . especially the birds! For some reason, I am connected to this way of living. It is what I took in through my pores as a child, growing up on sacred Indian ground.

This journey has been, and continues to be, a way of life that follows the path of what Joyce Rockwood Hudson terms "Natural Spirituality."[1] I am called to it by unseen forces that know what my soul needs. Christianity is a part of that journey, but, for me, as for Joyce Hudson and so many others, it is incomplete without this more mystical natural way: the wind in my face, the melody of the redwing that touches my heart, the dream character who amuses and enlightens me, the song of the rain outside my window, the thunder that speaks to me, the colorful rainbow, the warm sun on my back as I walk, and the synchronicity unfolding all around me.

These are elements of my spirituality that connect me to God . . . to the Great Creator. I want to live it daily, but it's not easy in this world of distractions and man-made doctrines. I want to stay connected to God in the most meaningful and loving way for me: through the lessons I am taught by the seen and unseen world . . . through dreamwork, synchronicity, and the way of the Native Americans and the mystics. I want to continue daily to learn how to walk with one foot in this outer world and one foot in the unseen world. I need this . . . as a complement to my traditional religious practices. One is the right hand and the other is the left. My soul needs both hands.

There are more than a dozen symbols or references in this dreamwork that are Native American in nature, including the INDIAN HEAD vision. Native Americans placed high value on dreams and visions, and also on synchronicity. So far, my work has taught me that dreams and synchronicity have made my Christian life stronger, not weaker. I am certain that the Holy Spirit chose this Native American guidance for me because it was the only frame of reference I had for understanding a spiritual system of living that includes dreams, meaningful coincidences, and the interweaving of the inner and outer worlds—a type of non-traditional "religion" or path that encompasses all aspects of our lives.

It helps me understand what is meant by "Sophia," or the feminine way of spirituality. I believe this is what Joyce is talking about when she speaks of "Natural Spirituality." In the WEARING OUT THE BATTERY dream, the dream helper holds her hands out to receive the contents I have to give her. Besides giving her the LEAKY BATTERY, I give her my SUNGLASSES/VISOR. Our dreams can sometimes be understood at the literal level by the masculine sun and its brilliant directness. But for the most part, dreams are illuminated and understood at a metaphorical level through the silvery-gold light of the feminine moon, as the dream of the INDIAN HEAD IN THE MOONLIGHT tried to tell me. This creative, indirect, metaphorical "language" is the same language of parables that Jesus so often used. It is the content or scripture, if you will, of a natural spirituality.

The pull to go back to my birthplace after finishing the first draft *was* an inner call, a call that I believe we all have: to return to our Real Home. This explains why my short course in dreamwork ended with the compelling desire to journey back to Mariemont, my birthplace and an ancient land of Native Americans, as well as symbolic of the inner journey home. Oh, I know I won't find the true home that I seek there. At times I have mistakenly thought the pull back *is* about going back to the houses of my childhood. But the dreams that have come to me this year, as I have done this rewriting, tell me otherwise. They continue to encourage me to let go of my attachments to those wood and brick homes, and to the memories they hold. This *pull* to those outer homes is but a metaphor for the real journey home . . . which is, and always has been, about returning to God, the Great Creator, and the loving Mother and Father of us all.

I hope this sharing of my journey will help you as you embark on a journey of your own. Sweet Dreams!

*I beseech almighty God out of his great grace and great courtesy to teach you himself.*

**The Cloud of Unknowing**[2]

# Twenty-Eight Lessons in Deciphering Dreams

The lessons I learned in this crash course about dreamwork are not exhaustive, but they have been helpful to me. By listing them here, I hope they will be helpful to you as you start your own dreamwork adventure.

*Lesson 1* **Mistakes.** Don't worry about making mistakes. Misinterpretations may happen for a reason.

*Lesson 2* **Morning Dreams.** The last dream of the night, the one near dawn, is usually the most coherent, complete, and helpful. It is the culmination, the summary, of what your unconscious mind has been working on all night with the help of the Holy Spirit. It is more important to rest than it is to wake up to record middle-of-the-night dreams.

*Lesson 3* **Messages.** Each night's dream contains a message. The message may pertain to that upcoming day or possibly to a situation that will occur days or months in the future. Sometimes, the message may clarify or build on something from the past. Reviewing the morning's dream and dreamwork after living the day can help you understand the message and a possible theme that may be emerging.

*Lesson 4* **Dream-Selves and Movement.** Dreams often contain three main characters: the learner or dreamself; an older, wiser spiritual self; and a younger self. The placement of the characters and the directions in which they move is significant. Moving up or down stairs or hills represents moving to "higher learning" or "down into the unconscious." The movements to the right, or objects on the right (of the dreamself), tend to signify something in the outer physical world. Movements to the left, or objects on the left, tend to signify the inner spiritual world.

*Lesson 5*    **Symbols.** Work with a dream symbol to elicit its many meanings: even *parts* of the symbol may be significant.

*Lesson 6*    **Open-ended Dreams.** Many dreams are left open-ended, unanswered, hanging in mid-air, with your dreamself feeling sad or confused. These dreams provoke thought and not only encourage ideas, but *action*. The dream conveys a message similar to Christ's parables.

*Lesson 7*    **Literal vs. Symbolic.** It helps to view a symbol, image, behavior, or situation from a literal point of view, then to examine it from a symbolic/metaphorical view. One view may or may not be more helpful than the other. It seems that the meanings are imbedded in the symbols; they are implicit, not explicit. Also, when the symbol is a person it is important to ask the questions, "How am I like him/her? How do I identify with him/her?"

*Lesson 8*    **Positive and Negative.** There is usually a positive and a negative aspect to symbols. Both should be examined when doing the dreamwork.

*Lesson 9*    **Gifts.** Symbols that evoke a moderate or strong feeling might refer to talents or spiritual gifts.

*Lesson 10*    **Dream Symbols are Personal.** Only the dreamer knows for sure what his or her own dream symbols represent. To try to interpret someone else's dreams might result in misinterpretation.

*Lesson 11* **Prophetic Dreams**. Occasionally, one of the words, part of an image or the image itself appears in the future in outer life. Seeing the symbol in a dream, then seeing it in outer life says "Pay attention!" to that special moment. It may give insight or lead to action.

*Lesson 12* **Forms.** Symbols come in different forms. They can appear as physical objects or they can come as something auditory such as music or spoken words.

*Lesson 13* **Consolation**. Symbols answer deep concerns, feelings, and questions from the prior day or even from the past.

*Lesson 14* **Themes**. Dreams often come in chapters. A theme may occur over several nights of dreaming, several weeks, or longer. The overall focus is to heal and instruct.

*Lesson 15* **Guidance**. Symbols can indicate when it is time to move on, and they help ease fears and anxiety over new changes.

*Lesson 16* **Strong Reactions.** Reacting strongly to a dream character or symbol by walking away, running, fighting, or ignoring it are clues to pay attention—something significant is emerging. After doing the dreamwork, meditating on the symbol that caused the strong reaction and asking it what it represents may reveal a whole area that needs to be examined and healed.

*Lesson 17* **Music**. Insight or meaning may come from music heard in your mind while awake. The words may relate to and interweave with an ongoing dream theme and speak to the issue at hand.

*Lesson 18* **Healing.** Sometimes the night's dream reveals just a small bit of something that needs healing or attention, but full exposure and the insight that follows may not unfold until the next day or two, maybe not even for weeks or months. Your mind may simply need time to process the content before gaining greater insight. During this time of processing, be aware of outer synchronistic signs, such as Bible passages, music, spoken words, or anything that can help give meaning to the unclear issue.

*Lesson 19* **Ask.** Ask a question. Pay attention. The Holy Spirit will answer. If the answer is in the form of a dream or vision with a luminous, awe-inspiring symbol, do not fail to ask, "What part of *me* does this represent?" — even if the symbol appears to be Jesus himself.

*Lesson 20* **Details.** When interpreting dreams, pay attention to the details—in the dream and in the dream notes. Details can help you understand patterns and connections, which can lead to incredible insight and guidance.

*Lesson 21* **Hold Back.** When working in groups or discussing dreams with others, share dreams, visions, and symbols, but, like the dream helpers, allow others to draw their own conclusions, as they are on their own path and must discover their own answers.

*Lesson 22* **Non-Judgmental Language.** When doing dreamwork, stay away from judgmental language, such as the words "right" and "wrong." It is more helpful to use "better," "best," or "not the best." This allows the dreamwork process to be one of gentle guidance, not of judgment and punishment.

*Lesson 23* **Circular Dreams**. Often a night's dream contains many themes that are part of a larger, overall theme. This type of dream seems to operate in a circle so the end and beginning can be reached from any starting point. The progression through the scenes comes "full circle" to the start.

*Lesson 24* **Outer Confirmation**. The outer physical world can confirm the learning of the inner world with synchronistic events. But, if the outer is strangely quiet (no synchronistic or meaningful experiences), or there are "stinky" problems like a skunk in the yard, or the computer crashes, look at the dream again, because the interpretation may be off course.

*Lesson 25* **Behavior as a Key**. Interpreting your dreamself's behavior may be the key to unfolding the rest of the dream symbols and scenarios.

*Lesson 26* **Truth**. You can't control a symbol if you really want the *truth*. The Holy Spirit gives you exactly what you need. If you can't decipher a symbol or dream after using dream techniques, ask the Holy Spirit to show you what the symbol means in another dream or meditation.

*Lesson 27* **Symbol and Metaphor Deciphering**. Dream language is, for the most part, a metaphorical language through which an issue in inner and/or outer life is presented. To decipher the dream's message, you need to understand the "language," which means think about what the story and its symbols represent for you. For example, in my dream story of the MOUNTAIN OF GARBAGE, I realized a two-fold message: with respect to my outer, physical world, I was supposed to revisit the emotional GARBAGE to help share my experience of healing with others; with respect to my inner, subconscious world, I was not meant to get rid of the GARBAGE as I had thought— it was a foundation for my inner growth and healing.

*Lesson 28*    **Insight.** Dream characters all have a gift to give. They reflect a part of you that needs to be recognized and brought to light. Those dream characters to which you have the strongest reaction have the most to reveal about your personality and how you look at life. If they are not especially likeable characters, exploring them will take away their power. Their origins, existence, and the function they serve may be revealed along with a new way for you to respond.

# PERMISSIONS

These pages constitute a continuation of the copyright page. Grateful acknowledgment is made to the following sources for permission to reprint material in their control:

Augsburg Fortress Publishers for an excerpt from *Tracing the Footsteps of God: Discovering What You Really Believe* by C.S. Song, copyright © 2007 by Fortress Press.

Broadman & Holman Publishers for an excerpt from *Believing God* by Beth Moore, copyright © 2004 by B&H Publishing Group.

HarperCollins Publishers for excerpts from *Dreams: God's Forgotten Language* by John Sanford, copyright © 1968 by John Sanford.

HarperCollins Publishers for excerpts from *The Sacred Journey* by Frederick Buechner, copyright © 1982 by Frederick Buechner.

HarperCollins Publishers for an excerpt from *Whistling in the Dark* by Frederick Buechner, copyright © 1983 by Frederick Buechner.

John Wiley & Sons, Inc. for an excerpt from *A Hidden Wholeness: The Journey Toward An Undivided Life* by Parker J. Palmer, copyright © 2004.

John Wiley & Sons, Inc. for an excerpt from *White China* by Molly Wolf, copyright © 2005.

NavPress Publishing Group for a scripture quotation from *The Message* by Eugene H. Peterson, copyright © 1993, 1994, 1995, 1996, 2000, 2001, 2002 by Eugene H. Peterson.

# *Endnotes*

## OPENING

1. *The Cloud of Unknowing*, Edited, with an introduction by James Walsh, S.J. (Mahwah, NJ: Paulist Press, 1981), p. 116.

## FOREWORD

1. These four books were the most helpful:
   Morton Kelsey,*Dreams: A Way To Listen To God* (New Jersey: Paulist Press, 1978);
   John Sanford, *Dreams: God's Forgotten Language* (New York, NY: HarperCollins, 1989);
   Louis M. Savary, Patricia H. Berne, Strephon Kaplan Williams, *Dreams and Spiritual Growth: A Judeo-Christian Way of Dreamwork* (Ramsey, NJ: Paulist Press, 1984);
   Jeremy Taylor, *Where People Fly and Water Runs Uphill: Using Dreams to Tap the Wisdom of the Unconscious* (New York, NY: Grand Central Publishing, 1993).

## INTRODUCTION

1. Hildegard of Bingen, *Illuminations of Hildegard of Bingen*, Text by Hildegard of Bingen, Commentary by Matthew Fox (Santa Fe, NM: Bear and Company, 1985), p. 76.

2. Psalm 57:1, *New Revised Standard Version Bible*, 1989, Division of Christian Education of the National Council of the Churches of Christ in the United States of America.

3. Parker J. Palmer, *A Hidden Wholeness: The Journey Toward An Undivided Life* (San Francisco, CA: Jossey-Bass, 2004), p. 1008.

4. Psalm 19:14, NRSV.

## Chapter Two
## A MATTER OF FAITH

1. Louis M. Savary, Patricia H. Berne, Strephon Kaplan Williams, *Dreams and Spiritual Growth: A Judeo-Christian Way of Dreamwork* (Ramsey, NJ: Paulist Press, 1984), p. 219.

2. John 15:7, NRSV.

3. Joan Borysenko, *A Woman's Journey to God: Finding the Feminine Path* (New York, NY: Riverhead Books, 1999), p. 76.

4. For an excellent discussion of the Greek concept of *chronos vs. kairos*, see Robert Farrar Capon, *The Romance of the Word: One Man's Love Affair with Theology* (Grand Rapids, MI: William B. Eerdmans Publishing Company, 1995), p. 47-50.

5. Jeremy Taylor, *Where People Fly and Water Runs Uphill: Using Dreams to Tap the Wisdom of the Unconscious* (New York, NY: Grand Central Publishing, 1993), p. 21.

6. Ibid, p. 239

7. J.M. Barrie, *Peter Pan* (New York: Charles Scribner's Sons, 1980), p. 137.

8. Beth Moore, *Believing God* (Nashville, TN: Broadman & Holman Publishers, 2004), p. ix.

9. Ibid, p. x.

10. Isaiah 43: 10, 1, 18, 4, NRSV.

## Chapter Three
## DREAMWORK TECHNIQUES

1. Frederick Buechner, *Whistling in the Dark: A Doubter's Dictionary* (New York, NY: HarperSanFrancisco, 1993), p. 41.

2. Psalm 51:6, *Evangelical Lutheran Worship* (Minneapolis, MN: Augsburg Fortress, 2006).

3. Lee Irwin, *Awakening to Spirit: On Life, Illumination, and Being* (Albany, NY: State University of New York Press, 1999), p. 94.

4. The books I found most helpful were the following:
   Morton Kelsey, *Dreams: A Way To Listen To God* (New Jersey: Paulist Press, 1978);
   John Sanford, *Dreams: God's Forgotten Language* (New York, NY: HarperCollins, 1989);
   Louis M. Savary, Patricia H. Berne, Strephon Kaplan Williams, *Dreams and Spiritual Growth: A Judeo-Christian Way of Dreamwork* (Ramsey, NJ: Paulist Press, 1984);
   Jeremy Taylor, *Where People Fly and Water Runs Uphill: Using Dreams to Tap the Wisdom of the Unconscious* (New York, NY: Grand Central Publishing, 1993).

5. *Where People Fly and Water Runs Uphill: Using Dreams to Tap the Wisdom of the Unconscious*, p. 11.

6. Ibid, p. 11.

7. *Dreams and Spiritual Growth*, p. 67-68.

8. Psalm 51:6,11,12, *Evangelical Lutheran Worship*.

9. Romans 8:28, NRSV.

## Chapter Four
## THE VOYAGE BEGINS

1. Christopher Bamford, *Earthly and Celestial Flowers* (an article in the Fall 2007 edition of *Parabola: Holy Earth*), p. 37. In this article, Mr. Bamford is retelling Novalis' story of the Blue Flower, which is a part of Novalis' unfinished novel *Henry of Oterdingen.*

2. Psalm 25:4, NRSV.

3. Kathleen Norris, *The Cloister Walk* (New York, NY: Riverhead Books, 1996), p. 156.

4. *The Access Bible: A Resource for Beginning Bible Students,* General Editors: Gail R. O'Day and David Peterson, (New York, NY: Oxford University Press, 1999), p. 409.

5. *Dreams and Spiritual Growth*, p. 5.

6. Cynthia Matyi Celtic Designs and Music, P.O. Box 9121, Cincinnati, Ohio 45209-0121, www.matyiart.com.

## Chapter Five
## MESSY, STINKY THINGS

1. Eugene H. Peterson, *Christ Plays In Ten Thousand Places: A Conversation In Spiritual Theology* (Michigan: Wm. B. Eerdmans, 2005), p. 197.

2. Ephesians 2:8-10, NRSV.

3. Morton Kelsey, *Dreams: A Way To Listen To God* (New Jersey: Paulist Press, 1978), p. 99.

### Chapter Six
### A BATHROOM BREAKTHROUGH

1. J. Phillip Newell, *Listening for the Heartbeat of God: A Celtic Spirituality* (New Jersey: Paulist Press, 1997), p. 103.

2. Acts 2:38, NRSV.

3. *Christ Plays In Ten Thousand Places,* p. 75.

4. Eckhart Tolle, *The Power of Now: A Guide to Spiritual Enlightenment* (Vancouver, B.C., Canada: Namaste Publishing, 2004), p. 77.

### Chapter Seven
### WORKING WITH SYMBOLS

1. Vine Deloria, *The World We Used to Live In: Remembering the Power of the Medicine Man* (Golden, Colorado: Fulcrum Publishing, 2006), p. 17.

2. 1 Corinthians 12:7, NRSV.

3. John Sanford, *Dreams: God's Forgotten Language* (New York, NY: HarperCollins, 1989), p. 181.

4. *Herders Dictionary of Symbols,* translated by Boris Matthews, (Wilmette, Illinois: Chiron Publications, 1986), p. 193.

### Chapter Eight
### A MESSAGE FROM THE PAST

1. Molly Wolf, *White China: Finding the Divine in the Everyday* (San Francisco, CA: Jossey-Bass, 2005), p. 119.

2. Isaiah 50:4, NRSV.

3. *Dreams: A Way to Listen to God*, p. 69.

4. Marcy Elter's book, *Singing the Moon into the Sky*, is available through a variety of online retailers.

## Chapter Nine
## LETTING GO OF GUILT

1. John Sanford, *Invisible Partners: How the Male and Female in Each of Us Affects Our Relationships* (New York: Paulist Press, 1980), p. 65.

2. 2 Corinthians 4:16, NRSV.

3. *Listening for the Heartbeat of God: A Celtic Spirituality,* p. 96-97.

4. *With One Voice*, "On Eagles Wings," (Minneapolis, MN: Augsburg Fortress, 1995), Text and Music by Michael Joncas, Hymn #779-780. Text and music copyright 1979 OCP Publications.

5. *Herders Book of Symbols*, p. 170.

6. Ibid, p. 171.

7. Ibid, p. 82.

## Chapter Ten
## THE RELIGION SQUEEZE

1. Madeleine L'Engle, *Herself: Reflections on a Writing Life,* compiled by Carole F. Chase, (Colorado Springs, CO: Waterbrook Press, 2001), p. 280.

2. Psalm 84:1-2, Eugene H. Peterson, *The Message: The New Testament Psalms and Proverbs In Contemporary Language,* (Colorado Springs, CO: Navpress, 1995), p. 664.

3. Luke 1:78-79, NRSV.

## Chapter Eleven
## DON'T BLOCK THE PROCESS!

1. Raimon Panikker, *The Experience of God: Icons of the Mystery*, (Minneapolis, MN: Augsburg Fortress, 2006), p. 141.

2. Joel 2:13, NRSV.

3. Sara Maitland, *A Big Enough God* (New York, NY: Riverhead Books, 1995), p. 143.

4. Carlos Castanada, *The Art of Dreaming* (New York, NY: HarperCollins, 1993), p. 22.

5. Joel 2:13, NRSV.

## CHAPTER TWELVE - RESCUING THE FEMININE

1. *Where People Fly and Water Runs Uphill: Using Dreams to Tap the Wisdom of the Unconscious*, p. 48-49.

2. 2 Corinthians 5:17, NRSV.

3. *Awakening to Spirit: On Life, Illumination, and Being*, p. 100.

4. My knowledge of interpretation of colors has come from many places. Two helpful books are *Herders Book of Symbols,* and *The Mystical Magical Marvelous World of Dreams* by Wilda B. Tanner. A helpful website for the symbolism of colors in the Christian Tradition is www.elca.org.

## Chapter Thireeen
## WHERE ARE YOU, JESUS?

1. A.W. Tozer, *The Radical Cross* (Camp Hill, PA: Wing Spread Publishers, 2005), p. 51.

2. Frederick Buechner, *The Sacred Journey* (New York, NY: Harper & Row, 1982), p. 96.

3. John 11:35, NRSV.

4. Julian of Norwich, *Julian of Norwich: Showings,* Translated from the critical text with an introduction by Edmund Colledge, O.S.A. and James Walsh, S.J., (Mahwah, NJ: Paulist Press, 1978), p. 196.

## Chapter Fourteen
## RESTORING THE BALANCE

1. *Herself: Reflections on a Writing Life,* p. 309.

2. Proverbs 8:32-35, NRSV.

3. *The Sacred Journey,* p. 111.

## Chapter Fifteen
## FINDING FEMININE WISDOM

1. *Where People Fly and Water Runs Uphill: Using Dreams to Tap the Wisdom of the Unconscious,* p. 46-47.

2. Wisdom of Solomon 9:10-11, *The Access Bible: A Resource for Beginning Bible Students,* "Apocryphal/ Deuterocanonical Books of the Old Testament" General Editors: Gail R. O'Day and David Peterson, (New York, NY: Oxford University Press, 1999), p. 64.

3. Robert Browning, excerpt from his poem "Paracelsus." Used with permission from Bartleby.com, Inc.

4. Karen Armstrong, *A History of God* (New York: Random House Publishing Group, 1993), p. 38. (The views expressed in this quote are Aristotle's not Karen Armstrong's.)

### Chapter Sixteen
### BLACK AND WHITE THINKING

1. *Christ Plays in Ten Thousand Places: A Conversation in Spiritual Theology*, p. 109.

2. Romans 12:2, NRSV.

3. *Dreams: God's Forgotten Language*, p. 156.

4. *A Big Enough God*, p. 179.

### Chapter Seventeen
### THE QUESTION

1. *The World We Used to Live In: Remembering the Power of the Medicine Men*, p. 107.

2. Wisdom of Solomon 7:7, 13,14, *The Access Bible: A Resource for Beginning Bible Students.*

3. *Christ Plays in Ten Thousand Places: A Conversation in Spiritual Theology*, p. 238.

### Chapter Eighteen
### LEARN WHAT'S "KEY"

1. *Dreams: A Way to Listen to God*, p. 100.

2. Hebrews 11:6, NIV.

3. *A Big Enough God*, p. 183.

### Chapter Nineteen
### AN ENDING AND A BEGINNING

1. Lee Irwin, *The Dream Seekers: Native American Visionary Traditions of the Great Plains* (Norman: University of Oklahoma Press, 1994), p. 52.

2. Psalm 63:7, NRSV.

3. Isaiah 55:6, NRSV.

4. *Listening for the Heartbeat of God: A Celtic Spirituality*, p. 35.

## Chapter Twenty
## AN ANCIENT CALL

1. *The World We Used to Live In: Remembering the Power of the Medicine Men*, p. 16.

2. Luke 11:9, 13, NRSV.

3. *Evangelical Lutheran Worship*, Hymn # 687 "Come to Us, Creative Spirit,"(Minneapolis, MN: Augsburg Fortress, 2006), Text by David Mowbray. Copyright 1979 Stainer & Bell, Ltd. (Admin. Hope Publishing Company, Carol Stream, IL 60188). All rights reserved. Used by permission.

4. *The Cloister Walk*, p. 62.

5. C.S. Song, *Tracing the Footsteps of God: Discovering What You really Believe* (Minneapolis, MN: Fortress Press, 2007), p. 132-133.

## EPILOGUE

1. Joyce Rockwood Hudson, *Natural Spirituality: Recovering the Wisdom Tradition in Christianity* (Danielsville, GA: JRH Publications, 2000), p. 3. Available from www.amazon.com.

2. *The Cloud of Unknowing*, p. 183.

DREAMS

DISCERNMENT
*Tink*
*Mom's Visit*
*The Indian Head Vision*
*The Monopoly Game/Indian Head*
*1440, 1440*
*The Flying Ship*
*The Labrador-Water Slide*
*Wearing Out the Battery*
*Breathing Under Water*
*The Medium Tilapia*
*The Monastery Gift*


FORGIVENESS
*The Treadmill*
*The Poopy Toddler*
*The White Truck*
*The Geisha*


UNDERSTANDING
*Pick Ten*
*Free Beef*
*Pyramid Toaster*
*Marcy's Home*
*On Eagle's Wings*
*Atop the J.C. Penney Store/Train Wreck*
*The Director's Chair*

# About the Author

Candy Smith is a retired children's protective service supervisor. During her twenty-two years in the field she wrote and received over fifteen grants. In the early 1970's, she co-authored two macrame craft booklets published by the Cunningham Arts Company, writing the text and sketching the instructions. She has been a monthly contributor to her Lutheran Church's newsletter, providing book reviews and articles, and she participates in Spirit Scribes - a writers' group at her church. Candy and her husband live in Ohio and between them they have four children and eight grandchildren.

CPSIA information can be obtained at www.ICGtesting.com
Printed in the USA
LVOW011148291111

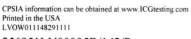

256951LV00005B/142/P

9 780982 827796